PROCLAMATION ON SINAI

Covenant and Commandments

⊕

PROCLAMATION ON SINAI

Covenant and Commandments

⊕

Valentin Tomberg

Angelico Press

First published in German in
Lazarus komm heraus!
as "Die Verkündung auf dem Sinai:
der Bund und die Gebote"
(Second of four separate texts) Hrsg. v. Kriele, Martin
© Verlag Herder Basel, Freiburg 1985
First English edition in *Covenant of the Heart*
Element Books, Rockport, MA, 1992
Second English edition, in *Lazarus Come Forth!*
Lindisfarne Books, Gt Barrington, MA 2006
Third English edition (as separate book)
newly-translated
Angelico Press, Brooklyn, NY 2022
English translation © James Wetmore 2022

For information, address:
Angelico Press
169 Monitor St.
Brooklyn, NY 11222
angelicopress.com

ISBN 978-1-62138-847-0 (pbk)
ISBN 978-1-62138-848-7 (cloth)
ISBN 978-1-62138-849-4 (ebook)

Cover Design: Michael Schrauzer

TABLE OF CONTENTS

Editor's Note

VALENTIN TOMBERG MAKES UNUSUAL DEMANDS on his readers in terms both of content and the spectrum of traditions, perspectives, and vocabularies he adopted over the course of his life. This means that, as regards any given book, some readers will be more familiar than others with its conceptual terrain: Anthroposophic, Hermetic, Kabbalistic, or Catholic.[1] As there is no way to supply sufficient terminological context to meet the needs of all possible readers, some pointers to useful sources are sometimes offered. All footnotes not otherwise attributed have been supplied by the editor. In the near future, Angelico Press will publish further works by Tomberg, to add to those already published.[2]

We acknowledge with warm appreciation Joel M. Park, to whom the Foreword owes its guiding theme, Richard Bloedon for his keen editorial assistance, and James Morgante, whose earlier translation of this text we were grateful

---

[1] "Catholic" in the sense of the Roman Catholic Church, but also (in Tomberg's late works especially) in the more extended sense of a truly Universal Church ("catholic" *means* "universal")—or, *Ecclesia universalis*. Tomberg does not employ this latter term; we propose it solely for the sake of a clear distinction.

[2] *Meditations on the Tarot: A Journey into Christian Hermeticism* (2019); *The Art of the Good: On the Regeneration of Fallen Justice* (2021); *Lazarus: The Miracle of Resurrection in World History* (2022); *Thy Kingdom Come: The New Evolution of the Good* (2022).

to have at hand as a guiding resource. And a further thanks goes to an ever-expanding circle of friends whose shared conviction of the pivotal importance of Tomberg's work has been a constant encouragement and support.

JAMES R WETMORE

Foreword

N HIS FINAL YEARS, VALENTIN TOMBERG WROTE four short works, which, after his death, were published together in German as *Lazarus komm heraus!*[1] The present book is the third of these late works (finished in May, 1972). The first (c.1967) of the four, *Thy Kingdom Come: The New Evolution of the Good*, was dedicated to his son Alex. (Its final essay, the "fourth work" referred to above, begun during this period but left unfinished, is included in this first book under the title *The Living Spirit-Breath: A Fragment.*) The second and longest of the four (1970), *Lazarus: The Miracle of Resurrection in World History*, has been published by Angelico Press.

These late writings, taken as a whole, may be seen as a "resurrection" of the Tomberg's "Our Father Course," given in the Netherlands (1940–1943), which elaborates in an astonishingly profound way on the seven petitions of the Lord's Prayer. For this reason, an excellent way to summarize and "situate" these last writings is to bring them into relation, text-by-text, with the theme of the seven petitions:

---

[1] Basel: Herder Verlag, 1985. In an earlier English translation, this text was published first as *Covenant of the Heart: Meditations of a Christian Hermeticist on the Mysteries of Tradition* (Rockport, MA: Element, 1992), and again later as *Lazarus Come Forth!* (Gt Barrington, MA: Lindisfarne Books, 2006).

PROCLAMATION ON SINAI

The first work, *Thy Kingdom Come: The New Evolution of the Good*, is clearly a meditation on the SECOND PETITION: "Thy kingdom come."

Lazarus: The Miracle of Resurrection in World History, which depicts, among other things, the intercessions of Christ's healing miracles in world history, may be seen as a further meditation on the THIRD PETITION: "Thy will be done, on earth as it is in heaven."

Proclamation on Sinai: Covenant and Commandments (the present work), is largely a study of the ten names of God, and thus a further meditation on the FIRST PETITION: "Hallowed be thy name."

The Living Spirit-Breath: A Fragment (included in the first volume, *Thy Kingdom Come...*) marks the beginning of an extended, but unfinished, meditation on the FOURTH PETITION: "Give us this day our daily bread." Here, "bread" is expanded into a symbol for nourishment as a whole, which, in its primal form as *Ruach Elohim*, can be called "breath," understood as spiritual, soul, and bodily nourishment: *panem supersubstantialem*.

In the very last of his writings just mentioned, Tomberg reaches back all the way to his very first intimation, as a small child, of the presence of God in the world, which he so movingly recalls in its Introduction:

> One day, sixty-eight years ago, when the author was four years old, he was sitting on a colored carpet playing with building blocks. Through an open window, he could see a cloudless blue sky. The child's mother was sitting in a chair, watching him at play. Suddenly the

child looked up, and, gazing through the window at the blue heavens, spontaneously asked his mother: "Where is God? Is he in heaven? Does he float there? Or is he sitting there? Where?"

The child's mother sat up straight and gave the following answer, which has held true for the child ever after: "God is present everywhere. We know that, even though we cannot see the air, it penetrates every-thing—and that it is only thanks to the air that we can live and breathe. In this same way, we live and breathe in God. And since it is in God that we live and breathe, it is from God and thanks to God that we live."

This answer, so clear and convincing, was like a breath of fresh air that ever after blew away any conun-drums on this question, leaving behind always the cer-tainty of God's invisible presence everywhere. And as has been said, this seed-thought was to flourish into the heights and depths and breadths, proving to be the pri-mal seed from which a many-branched tree of insight and faith unfolded over the following decades of the author's life.

We are most fortunate that these precious works, these "res-urrections" of the worthy gleanings of Tomberg's personal path of destiny during the twilight of his earthly life, are being made available in this time of pitched conflict between the powers of good and evil. Our guiding hope in presenting this series is that some readers may resolve to take up the thread of Tomberg's life-mission; for clearly, the last work in this series ended abruptly. What if we were to take further his interrupted meditations on "breath" and "bread"? What if we were to ponder further in the same spirit, in solitude or in community, the fifth, sixth, and seventh petitions of the Lord's Prayer, for which he left no corresponding final meditations?

When considering our own lives, we may well ask: What in *my* past is worthy of resurrection? And, as for the worthy gleanings granted me in my earthly life, have I offered these up to the resurrecting power of Christ and thus to the "Church" in its fullest sense as the *Ecclesia universalis*? Let us widen our vision so that we also may hear ringing, throughout all times and in all places, the resounding call: *Lazarus, Come Forth!*

INTRODUCTION

The Cloud Over the Mountain

XODUS, THE SECOND BOOK OF MOSES, DEPICTS the world-historic event of the revelation and proclamation of the Decalogue, or ten commandments. There we read how a thick cloud covered Mt. Sinai, and thunder and lightning accompanied that proclamation: The people remained at a distance, while Moses approached the "thick darkness where God was." (Exodus 20:21)

Afterward, Moses emerged from the darkness of the cloud that covered the mountaintop, descended, and proclaimed the divine commandments to the people in their own language and voice. A cloud heavy with revelation lay over the mountain, and Moses "precipitated" this cloud into the ten proclamations of the Decalogue. These proclamations were the humanly comprehensible and accessible *crystallization* of what had taken place in the "thick darkness where God was." Further, in keeping with the principle of divine correspondence, the thunder and lightning were translated or concretized into human language in the form of the ten commandments. This is clearly indicated in the biblical text itself; regarding the hallowing of the sabbath, we read therein:

> For in six days the LORD made heaven and earth, the sea, and all that is in them, and rested the seventh day;

1

therefore the LORD blessed the sabbath day and hallowed it. (Exodus 20:11)

Here the celestial-divine correspondence underlying the fourth commandment, to hallow the sabbath, is expressly indicated: *the celestial-divine archetype of the seventh day of creation is to be reflected in the earthly-human realm.* Herewith the Bible provides the key to understanding the mystery of the cloud upon the mountain: it contained within it the divine-cosmic correspondences of the ten commandments intended for the earthly-human realm. Figuratively speaking, the ten commandments can be seen as "precipitations" of the corresponding archetypes that were contained within the cloud upon the mountain. Furthermore, just as the fourth commandment of the Decalogue represents the earthly-human correspondence of such an archetype, so also (as we shall see) do all the other commandments correspond to *their* respective archetypes.

The Decalogue is an organic whole, a holism. Just now we pointed out that all ten commandments are earthly-human correspondences, or reflections, of cosmic-divine archetypes, and also that each commandment may be regarded as the precipitation of one of those archetypes. But what must be further emphasized is that the divine-archetypal content corresponding to *all ten commandments* was present *in the same one cloud* upon the mountain. And since the proclamation of the Decalogue was not a matter of human but of *divine* law-giving, its establishment must not be sought in the earthly-human realm of human morality or social relationships, but in the cosmic-divine world-order: in the "cloud" that lay *above* the mountain. The Decalogue, then, must be regarded as the earthly-human reflection of the *moral world-order.* Accordingly, to under-

stand and fittingly appreciate the *individual* commandments, we must first climb with Moses, in spirit, to the top
of Mt. Sinai, and enter there into the darkness of the cloud
"in which God was." Only if we are able to retranslate the
words chiseled upon the stone tablets into the primal language of thunder and lightning in which they were first
proclaimed, will we ever fully grasp that the ten commandments are actually of *divine origin*.

THE
HOLISM OF THE
DECALOGUE

"I am Yahweh, your God"

The Unity of the Decad

"I am the LORD, your God, who brought
you out of Egypt, out of the land of slavery."
Exodus 20:2

LL TEN COMMANDMENTS OF THE DECALOGUE
presuppose *one foundational commandment*: to
acknowledge the revelation of the LORD (YAH-
VEH) *as* such. To better understand how the ten
commandments reflect the divine world-order and claim
origin in the One God, let us cast a first glance into the
Hebrew esoteric tradition:

> Ten are the (qualitative) numbers of the ineffable
> sefirot. Ten, and not nine. Ten, and not eleven. Learn
> this wisdom, and be wise in the understanding of it.
> Investigate these numbers, and draw knowledge from
> them. Fix the design in its purity, and pass from it to
> its Creator seated on his throne. . . . These ten sefirot
> which are ineffable, whose appearance is like scintil-
> lating flames, have no end, but are infinite. The word

5

of God is in them as they burst forth, and as they
return; they obey the divine command, rushing along
as a whirlwind, returning to prostrate themselves at
his throne.[1]

So is it written in the *Sepher Yetzirah*, the Book of Creation,
the oldest document of the Hebrew esoteric tradition, the
Kabbalah.

Though opinions vary widely as to its age, all agree that
the *Sepher Yetzirah* antedates the *Zohar*, the Book of Splendor,
dor, which contains the most comprehensive account of the
teachings of the Kabbalah, and whose origin is placed in
the thirteenth century after Christ. In any case, the *Sepher
Yetzirah* is beyond doubt an ancient and authentic source
of the Hebrew esoteric tradition and faithfully transmits its
fundamental teachings. Among these teachings belongs,
first and foremost, that of the *qualitative* meaning of number.
ber. According to this teaching (which was also that of the
Pythagoreans), numeration does not consist of an unlimited
synthetic series of increments by one, but of a progressive
analysis of oneness. Oneness, or unity, encompasses all
numbers; and in the end, all numbers are meant to be led
back to oneness. Thus, numeration consists of two operations:
tions: analysis of oneness by reducing it to its constituent
elements, followed by synthesis of these constituent elements
ments (i.e., resolving them into oneness again by apprehending
hending them together as a unity).

Application of this method of synthesis to the elements
of reductive analysis is the essence of intellectual knowledge,
edge, which we could just as well call "becoming conscious

---

[1] Sefaria Community translation.

of unity in differentiation." Put another way, the full cycle of numeration consists of two parts: first, the qualitative elements or numbers implicit in oneness are made explicit; then these elements or numbers are resolved back into their original unity through synthetic cognitive vision.

In accord with this qualitative understanding of number, the first commandment ("I am the Lord your God, who brought you out of the land of Egypt, out of the house of bondage; you shall have no other gods before me") is, as the first-numbered, the one, or oneness, underlying all ten commandments. Ten is one divided into a decad; and the well-known 613 precepts of the Torah simply represent a further analysis of the ten commandments through the principle of "explication."

Reduction to ten, or oneness, is called "theosophical addition," where numbers are added horizontally. In our present case of 613, this "lateral sum" would be $(6 + 1 + 3) =$ 10. Now, although ten is of course also a figure, among others, in the analytic differentiation of oneness, in its special case the initial oneness is not lost to view amid the other numbers that are later made explicit through analysis; on the contrary, in this special case of ten, it is far more a matter of oneness remaining *implicit* in it. As the *Sepher Yetzirah* says:

> These ten sefirot which are, moreover, ineffable, have their end, even as their beginning, conjoined, even as is a flame to a burning coal: for our God is superlative in his unity, and does not permit any second one. And who canst thou place before the only one?[2]

[2] Ibid.

7

Thus, even as the flame is "conjoined" to the burning coal, so is oneness discernible in the ten. In the ten, beginning and end coincide. This is why, in the qualitative mathematics of the ancients, ten was considered one, just as twenty was considered two, thirty was considered three, etc.

In this qualitative milieu, numbers carry the significance of concepts, ideas, and ideals, and not merely of numeration. Here ONE signifies oneness (*monad*), unity; TWO signifies twoness (*dyad*), polarity, opposition, discord; THREE signifies threeness (*triad*), peace, reconciliation of the conflict of duality; FOUR signifies fourness (*tetrad*), the quaternity of causality (*causa efficiens, causa formalis, causa materialis, causa finalis*); FIVE signifies fiveness (*pentad*), making use of causality, creative work on the basis of primary causes, the principle of *freedom*; SIX signifies sixness (*hexad*), the principle of choosing between two opposing directions; SEVEN signifies sevenness (*heptad*), the chooser, the individuality; EIGHT signifies eightness (*ogdoad*), righteousness or harmony between the twin *tetrads* of higher and lower causality; NINE signifies nineness (*ennead*), the triple peace of the threefold surmounting of opposites; TEN signifies again the original oneness (*monad*) in the tenness (*decad*).

In this sense, the ten commandments may indeed be likened to ten flaming tongues of one and the same fire: *the commandment to acknowledge the revelation of the Lord.*

THE
FIRST
COMMANDMENT

"You Shall Have No
Other Gods Before Me"
Exodus 20:3

The Commandment of Essentialism

UMANITY IS FACED WITH THE CHOICE BETWEEN two principal orientations: toward empirical *existence*, and toward *essence* or *being*. Depending on how we choose, we become either an *existentialist* or an *essentialist*. We are either "orphaned" *from* our ground of being, or we turn all our yearning and striving *toward* our ground of being.

The essentialist is "alone, but not lonely." The existentialist is *not* "alone" (that is, he must inevitably share with others the existential necessities of life and destiny), yet *is* "lonely," for he knows no higher reality than his own empirical self, which, together with other selves, seems simply to have been tossed into existence. Even if, for political, social, or humanitarian reasons, an existentialist should join this or that group of others of similar persuasion, for all practical purposes he will remain isolated. For loneliness is not absence of society but a *condition* in which the empirical self is for us the highest and final level there is, beyond and behind which is nothing at all. Those for whom the empirical self serves as center and apex of their soul life cannot know the sphere of being above the self—the sphere whence their self first emerged, and which remains ever its home.

The empirical self is only a *mental image*, compounded of bodily impressions (and memories thereof) along with temperament, character, and inclinations, all knit together into a comprehensive *abstraction*. This empirical self is very different from our *real* self, our *center of being*, which we may characterize as the rememberer in our remembering, the thinker in our thinking, the feeler in our feeling, the willer in our willing.

This real self at the center of our being is not an abstract mental image, but the concrete reality of the inner identity at our core—that which threads together our life experiences into one continuous tapestry. Our real self (not some mental image of it) is the inner "lord" that stands *above* the ever-shifting conditions of our soul life (with its moods, inclinations, wishes, and kaleidoscope of mental images), and that, for the most part, rules over them. This real self is the centerpoint of our soul life, its invariable core. It is a fragment of *being* fixed within the tumult of our soul's mutable existence. Our real self, then, stands at the threshold of two worlds: the world of external existence and the world of being-above-the-self.

Whereas the existentialist experiences the self in its relation to the external world, the essentialist experiences the self in relation to the world of being-above-the-self. For the existentialist, the self is the experiential *terminus* or final outcome of interiorizing the existential world. For the

10

essentialist, the self is the *point of departure* for an "exodus" into the realm of Being. This latter is the path taken by those intent on becoming ever more essential. Angelus Silesius meant this path when he said: "Man, become essential!" This "becoming essential" begins with the self, and progresses then through stages of increasing depth and inwardness, until it arrives at what is both the final and the first inwardness: Being, itself, as the source of self—or, *God*. God is not *external* to the self, but is above—transcends— the self. God is the most inward of the inward. God is more inward even than the sanctuary of our own self: for just as our own *self* is inner "lord" of our own *soul*, so is *God* LORD of *all selves*. This is what St. Augustine meant when he said of God:

> You were more inward to me than my most inward
> part and higher than my highest.[1]

This saying offers a characterization, both concise and plenary, of the essentialist's underlying attitude toward the reality of what lies above the self. For the essentialist, God is not a thing, not an object of knowledge or belief that stands over against (or, face-to-face) with a knowing subject or faithful seeker. No, He is beyond and above any such separation of subject and object: God transcends both what is objective and what is subjective.

The certitude of God's reality that we call "faith" is not founded upon empiricism, or upon any proof supposed to take its start from empirical reality. Faith is the *effect* on our self of the reality of God-above-the-self. God's reality makes

---

[1] *Confessions* 3.6.11.

11

itself known by a *breath* moving through our self, like a homeward wind. This is not knowledge, for no object is thereby known by a knowing subject. It would be more true to say that it is the self, the subject, that is known (or, cognitively permeated) by higher Being. The self becomes an object of the all-pervasive cognition of One who is higher, who transcends the self. From the first moment when we awaken to consciousness, this certainty of *being known by God* exists within us. This is also the fundamental tenet of the epistemological teaching of Franz von Baader, a deeply religious thinker who may be considered representative of the spiritual stream of essentialism.

This fundamental tenet of the spiritual stream of essentialism teaches us, as we have said, that just as the self is both center and "lord" (*kyrios*) of our soul, so God is both center and LORD (*kyrios*) of the self, and center of all selves. God as Sun of eternal Being sends forth His rays of essence into existence, and these rays of essence—as present in existence—are no other than individual selves fashioned in His image and likeness.

Just as the *soul* (with its powers of thinking, feeling, and will) "acknowledges as its lord the self and its revelation," which is *conscience* (except in cases of madness, moral idiocy, or intoxication), so does the *self* "acknowledge as its LORD the God-above-the-self and His revelation," which is *the conscience of consciences* (for this revelation stands *above* individual conscience). And it is precisely this conscience of consciences, towering above the individual self and its personal conscience, that, when experienced and recognized as such, is worshipped as *holy* by the self, and also by the powers of the soul subordinated to the self. What is holy to the self is, then, on the one hand, something that is not dissimilar to it by nature, and, on the other, something experienced as towering above it and far surpassing it.

The guiding principle of essentialism is *alignment with the holy*, with worshipping the God-above-the-self. As such, it is not a matter of aligning with or worshipping the god alongside or external to the self—and never mind the god below the self! The holy is not to be sought and found in the realm of empirical existence, but in the realm of *Being*: that Being which towers above the self.

⊕

Now, the *horizontal* of empirical existence (all that which spatial extension and temporal succession have to offer) can divert and hinder us on the *vertical* of the path to the God-above-the-self. This is why the revelation of God as Being (Exodus 3:14–15)—as both I AM THE I AM and THE ONE WHO IS[2]—must be *preceded* by an "exodus" from the "house of bondage," an exodus from the polytheistic influences of untold gods laying claim on our piety.[3] Yes, such a revelation must surely be preceded by a "wandering through the desert." That is why the revelation on Mt. Sinai had to come *after* the exodus out of Egypt (and after the subsequent wanderings).

Egypt at that time was a catch-all of cultic attachments to the elemental powers of empirical existence, both in space

---

[2] It is important to establish clarity of nomenclature at the outset, according to the author's usage. Regarding the revelation to Moses on Mt. Horeb, EHIYEH ASHER EHIYEH is here given as above (I AM THE I AM), whereas LORD (that is, YHVH, or "He is") is most often given as THE ONE WHO IS (in accordance with the author's use of the German *Das Seiende,* "That which exists," for this name).

(sun, moon, and stars) and time (fertility, procreation, life and death, natural evolution)—that is, of devotion directed solely to natural powers representing a full spectrum of the *compulsive* aspects of existence.

But Egypt was a house of bondage not solely on account of the compulsory labor exacted from the Israelites by their masters; this was also (and especially) because the form of worship pervading the land entailed a pleading for the necessities of life from "gods" of empirical existence. For this reason, the exodus of the Israelites out of Egypt was a revolutionary event without precedent. Consider for a moment: a great multitude chose to go into the desert to offer sacrifice to a God not present *anywhere* in the realm of empirical existence, whose name meant THE ONE WHO IS! This unprecedentedness was, in fact, precisely Pharaoh's view of the desert exodus.

To make clear the unprecedented audacity of the proposal Moses put to Pharaoh, we would have to imagine several hundred thousand workers in Soviet Russia petitioning the Politburo for a furlough to spend time in the Gobi desert. This would *not* be for the purpose of devoting themselves to the "absolute truth" of dialectical materialism, or of worrying themselves about ways and means to maximize produc-

---

[3] Then Moses said to God: "If when I come to the people of Israel and say to them, 'The God of your fathers has sent me to you,' and they ask me, 'What is His name?' What shall I say to them?" God said to Moses: "I AM THE I AM [EHIYEH ASHER EHIYEH, אהיה אשר אהיה]." God (ELOHIM, אלהים) spoke further to Moses: "Say this to the people of Israel, 'The LORD ("He is," YHVH, יהוה), the God (ELOHIM) of your fathers, the God of Abraham, the God of Isaac, and the God of Jacob, has sent me to you. This is My name forever, and thus I am to be remembered throughout all generations.'" AUTHOR

tivity, or to more seamlessly indoctrinate the young in communistic theories, and the like. Instead, it would be for the purpose of devoting themselves—there in the wilderness, as far as may be from collective farms, communes, factories, and the surveillance of the omnipotent Party apparatus—to contemplating the God-above-the-self, who is more *essential* than anything to do with communism and capitalism or the means of production and the dictatorship of the proletariat! Just as the Soviets would surely have rejected such an audacious petition as madness, so too did Pharaoh reject the Israelites' petition. Truly, totalitarian regimes of three millennia ago hardly differ from those of our time. Indeed, in all important respects, the house of bondage of our time is the same as that of the time of Moses.

But the reality of our present house of bondage is far broader and more far-reaching than just the sociopolitical state apparatus: its signature is in every form of thought or belief that is to any degree tinged with *determinism*. Whenever we hold to the belief that chains of causality—set in motion in the past—inexorably determine not only present events but also all *future* events, we are confined within this house of bondage. Whenever we subscribe to the belief that no "uncaused" cause can be found such as might strike like lightning from the realm of moral-spiritual freedom into the prevailing world of causality, we are inmates within the walls of this deterministic house of bondage.

Further, belief in determinism is tantamount to *dis*belief in miracles. And whoever does not believe in miracles—and therefore does not believe in the irruption of *new* causes from the moral-spiritual into the existential realm—is *ipso facto* caught in this deterministic house of bondage. Prisoners of this house of bondage hold, for example, that heredity is more powerful than spiritual-moral freedom. For them, heredity is a god before whom they bow down. Thus speaks the determinist: "We are determined by heredity; heredity created us."

Then again, other prisoners of the deterministic house of bondage look to stellar influences (say, in the birth horoscope) as the causal agents of our destinies. For them the stars also are gods before whom they bow down. As for those who worship natural evolution as a goddess (and their number is legion), they hold that with the aid of its twin protagonists—the struggle for existence and the survival of the fittest—natural evolution contrived to transmogrify an intricate system of nerves and brain into what is called the human being (*homo sapiens*). Those who think this way also bow down before the gods of existence. They do not worship the God-above-the-self. Instead, they worship forces *outside* and *beneath* the self—forces "above in heaven," "below on the earth," or "in the water under the earth."

All who hold such views as we have mentioned here are "in Egypt, in the house of bondage," for they serve the gods of existence and do not acknowledge THE ONE WHO IS, the God of Being. They have not as yet set forth from the house of bondage into the desert to experience there the reality of the God-above-the-self, whose name is THE ONE WHO IS. The encounter with the reality of the God-above-the-self is possible only in the "desert," only beyond the sphere of influence of the other "gods": the gods of *existence*.

This is why the first commandment of essentialism proclaims that to acknowledge the God of Being, the God-above-the-self, *precludes* acknowledging any other gods (*elohim aherim*) next to Him. As THE ONE WHO *IS*, God has claim on our *being*, on our own selves—that is, on the *undi-*

vided devotion of the center and essence of *every aspect* of our consciousness.

Now, this claim on our undivided devotion is not satisfied when, for example, such disproportionate prominence is ascribed to the sex drive, or *libido*, that the phenomena of spiritual and cultural life are regarded as little, if anything, more than sublimations of that drive. Far from worshipping the God of Being, those who have fallen victim to this obsession are instead worshipping the ancient goddess Venus (known also as Aphrodite or Astarte), who dominates their every thought and deed. Such people are indeed worshippers of the goddess Venus, no matter how scientifically enlightened they may otherwise believe themselves to be.

Then there are others among the "well-informed" who believe they have located the driving force of evolution in the *struggle for existence*, and the conflicts of class and race that follow from it. Those obsessed in this way are in truth worshippers of Mars.

Thus the ancient gods reappear disguised in the present! Even inhuman Moloch is back again in the guise of *collectivism*, still demanding human sacrifice as in olden days. Are not collectives (whether of state, national, or class origin) demanding, yet again, that we sacrifice our "firstborn": our heritage, our hereditary rights? In the final analysis, collectives always demand the sacrifice of our individualism. Does not the ancient Phoenician cult of the Canaanites and the Carthaginians live robustly on today in the "worship" of state, party, and national collectives?

Lest our stance on the matters detailed above may seem overwrought, we hasten to emphasize that, for us, the point is not whether such "other gods" actually do correspond "in some way" to existential reality, but that they do not "proceed from" the spheres above the self. They proceed, rather, from the existential spheres *beneath* and *outside* the self. They enslave the self and impede its way to true freedom: to freedom in God, to freedom in He who "is more myself than I myself am." Such "other gods" do not lie on the essential-izing vertical of ever-increasing inwardization—that is, on the trajectory from subjective conscience to objective good, from individual self to the fountainhead whence every self shines forth.

God is not just "one phenomenon" among others. *God is the fountainhead of selfhood!* He is more intimate, more inward, than the most intimate and inward we know: our own self. For this reason, even taken together, the entirety of the phenomenal world, of the conceptual world of men-tal images, and of language (to the degree that it conforms to these things) does *not* suffice to know the God-above-the-self and to bring Him to expression! Only in the *language of the self,* which is the language of conscience, can we conceive of and speak about God. Only in this language can the first and fundamental commandment of essential-ism as proclaimed by Moses be heard, understood, and acknowledged:

> I am the LORD (*anochi* YHVH), thy God (*elohecha*),
> who brought you out of the land of Egypt, out of the
> house of bondage. (Exodus 20:2)

In other words: "I am THE ONE WHO IS, who stands above your self, who has freed you from the bondage of existence. That is why you should not fall back into the bondage of existence by subordinating your self to the *forces* of existence!" Or, as Moses records it:

> You shall have no other gods besides me. (Exodus 20:3)

No such "other god" can pose an alternative to THE ONE WHO IS! All such "other gods" relate to the God-above-the-self as periphery does to center, as relative to absolute, as existence to essential being. There is as little choice in this matter as there could be any choice in everyday experience between the reality of the self and that of wind, or rain, or any other force of the external world.

Wind and rain are peripheral, nonessential. The self's voice of conscience is central, essential. We do not *choose* between the peripheral and the central, the nonessential and the essential—we *discriminate*. And the same is true of the first commandment: for here also it is not a matter of choice between the nonessential and the essential, but of discrimination. *Whoever makes this discrimination has already chosen.* However, such discrimination calls upon both head and heart, not head alone—for there remains at all times a lingering danger of falling away from the God-above-the-self who reveals Himself as the conscience of the world. The danger stems from remaining susceptible to the correlative temptation to worship a god *beneath* and *outside* of the self, an "other god."

⊕

Is this not exactly how matters turned out at the close of Moses's forty-day sojourn on the summit of Mt. Sinai in dialogue with the voice of God—that is, with the conscience of the world? Those at the mountain's foot fell away, following the collective will of the people (the *volonté générale* of Jean-Jacques Rousseau, the *vox populi* or *vox dei*) —to which Aaron also succumbed. They gathered donations of gold jewelry, out of which was cast the "golden calf," the idol of a golden bull. With respect to this archetype of falling away, it was not merely a matter of preference for the sensible and concrete over the suprasensible and purely moral. No, something far deeper and far more significant than preference was at work. It was in fact a rebellion of the collective will of the people against the aristocratic-hierarchical order that Moses stood for.

Moses *proclaimed* what was revealed to him on top of Mt. Sinai. He did not *interpret* the collective will of the people that had awoken in those assembled at its foot. This latter was done by the subsequent high priest Aaron, who during the forty-day absence of his younger brother Moses had to take upon himself the responsibility of leading the people. While Moses stood high on the mountaintop before the face of the revelatory God, Aaron stood at its foot before the face of the collective will of the people. Moses translated the divine revelation into the language of human concepts and ideas; Aaron translated the content of the people's collective will into this same language of the people, but in terms associated instead with cultic worship of the divine. This is what led to the singing and dancing of the people around the statue of the golden calf.

What need, we may ask, what yearning of the collective will of the people, was satisfied in this way? In a certain sense, it also was an aspiration for "something higher," but in the guise of a proto-democratic aspiration; for the "something higher" they desired to worship and obey was to be something that they themselves had chosen to create or to project from the resources of their own collective will. To their way of thinking, if this "something higher" were of their *own* devising, and embodied their *own* primal collective will, then whatever authority it might wield would be assured to derive solely from its role as a representation of their collective will. They wanted to base the prerogatives of a higher authority *not* upon a "dogmatically" proclaimed revelation (such as Moses received and communicated), but upon their *own* will—their *collective* will. Since the convincing power of such a collective "something higher" could derive *solely* from that power's presence or operation in *all* the people, its directives (by contrast to the "Thou shalt..." of the ten commandments) would start with the words "We want..." This is how it came to pass that the "conscience of God"—as revealed to the chosen few and proclaimed by them—came to be superseded by the "god of the will."

Now, as is all too well known, the weight of conscience can be a most onerous burden. In the story of Moses on Mt. Sinai, the people's relief at having this burden lifted is portrayed by their jubilant dance around the golden statue. Through their collective will, the people had not only *chosen* their own god as overlord, but had actually *created* it. The democratizing freedom, or license, of the collective will of the people went that far! "This is the god that led us out of Egypt," professed the people at the altar of the god of their own collective will. "It is the collective will of the people, *our* national god and overlord, that has led us out of Egypt." Such was the belief and profession of faith (Exodus 32:4) taken up, as of one accord, by the people as they danced around the golden statue at Mt. Sinai's foot. This belief and this profession of faith resulted from entirely democratic proceedings, for it rested upon the people's resolve to provide their *own* highest authority; and, having done so, to pledge to it their allegiance.

It must be admitted, then, that what transpired in the forming of the people's decision to favor a god of their own collective will was undertaken entirely in the spirit of dem-

21

ocratic freedom. But behind this *seemingly* democratic proceeding lay a deeply hidden significance and intention—a motive aligned, instead, with the laws of what we may call "the technology of magic." As forerunner of scientific technology, magic shares the latter's goal of extending human will over nature—including over our own human nature.

Of course, magic has its own mechanics and laws, just as science does. In our day, for instance, the computer (a machine invented by "the people") has come to play an ever more pervasive role in our everyday lives by virtue of its capacity to solve problems and answer questions—a capacity in this respect not so unlike that of the sacred oracles of antiquity. Computers carry out their protocols on the basis of such elements of human will and intelligence as have been programmed into them; similarly, long ago, in such cases as the fashioning of the golden calf, elements of human will and intelligence were "programmed" into entities (both visible and invisible) which thereafter came to be worshipped as overlords. The collective will of the people was thus "projected" into such collectively-created entities, animating them. And the greater the potency of the collective will and phantasy invested in the people's creations, the more effective and powerful the dominion of these creations over them would be.

⊕

Let us turn now to the fundamental magical law at work in the creation and animation of such overlords[4] as we are

---

[4] German: *Führer* ("leaders"). In the context of collective will, this term quite possibly bears the more nefarious connotation of Hitler's role as *Führer* of the German people during the Nazi period.

speaking of—that is, of "existential" gods (called *egregores* in the French magical tradition). According to this magical law, there must be present in their formation first of all a collective will—which, by means of collective, intellectual phantasy deriving from it, conjures an image (whether mental picture or external idol) compounded of collective contributions, offerings of valuables, jewelry, etc. More specifically, the resulting mental picture or external idol must be an amalgamation of *voluntary* contributions from all members of the community concerned (nation, brotherhood, party, etc.). In the case of an external idol meant to epitomize and embody the collective will, all must donate gold, silver, or whatever other precious materials may be most prized by the community. And the more offerings brought forward from which to create the idol, the greater its potency and authority will be. Whether external idol or mental picture, such an "overlord" must be intensively enlivened, animated, "magnetized" (French: *aimanté*) in order to become magically effective—for the energy they discharge in influencing the collective disposition of the people (to the extent even of healing their illnesses) will be proportionate to the psychic energy stored up in them. And to retain their effectiveness, such collectively-generated external idols or mental pictures must be regularly recharged, rather as an electric battery is. Such recharging is accomplished through repeated enactments of the cult attached to them, culminating in sacrificial offerings of highly valued articles, and animals—and, in certain places (such as Mexico and Carthage), even human beings.

This magical law of creating a god, and thereafter ensuring its continued effectiveness, was followed to the letter by the people of Israel at the foot of Mt. Sinai. First, they made known their collective will, to which Aaron felt obliged to acquiesce (for he dared not oppose his *individual* will to their *collective* will). Then, they fabricated an external embodiment (idol) of their collective will, which not only represented this will symbolically, but epitomized and precipitated it. All the people donated golden jewelry, which was melted down and recast in the figure of a bull. An altar was then erected in front of the idol, where animal sacrifices were offered as the people danced around, praising it in song—thereby collectively magnetizing it further.

Now, as regards Moses's subsequent reversal of this magical process, it is important to note that, after coming down from the mountain, shattering the stone tablets to pieces, and having three thousand of the people slain in punishment by the Levites, Moses even further reversed the magical process to which the people's collective will had succumbed (in the fabrication of their god) by *pulverizing* the idolatrous golden calf and then compelling the people to drink water in which the resulting powder had been dissolved. By this means, what the people's collective will had projected out of itself was quite literally reabsorbed by them.

⊕

Now, falling away from the revealed and proclaimed God in favor of a collectively self-chosen and fabricated god, as depicted in the Bible, is the archetype that presides over *every* instance of falling away from the truths of revelation in favor of collective will. Most often, this falling away is expressed as an appeal from the people for "more engagement" with the "spirit of the times." Whenever such an appeal is yet again voiced, yet another "Aaron" yields to it and yet another "Moses" remonstrates by shattering to pieces the "stone tablets" of the timeless law, whereafter (when the people have soberly realized the error of their ways) the stone tablets are yet again rewritten by the revelatory God—but without altering one iota of the original, timeless revelation.

Yet again today, under pressure from the collective will of various groups "of the people," we find within the Church this same archetype of falling away from timeless tradition. Here again, we find many another "yielding Aaron," and likewise many another "shattering Moses" whose all-too-human first response is to smash to pieces the tablets of the timeless law entrusted to his care. What else does excommunication really amount to but a repeated shattering of the stone tablets of the timeless law as regards those who have fallen away? Any reform which over its long history the Church has not enacted for the purpose of enriching understanding of revealed truths or of ennobling morals, but solely to mollify appeals from the collective will of the people of the Church, serves only to replicate Aaron's deed. On the other hand, however, any reform enacted over the millennia by the Church for the sole purpose of deepening and intensifying life within the frame of transmitted revelation replicates the *restoration* of the first stone tablets that Moses shattered to pieces:

> The tablets were the work of God, and the writing was the writing of God, graven upon the tablets. . . . The Lord said to Moses: "Cut two tablets of stone like the first, and I will write upon the tablets the words that were on the first tablets." (Exodus 32:16, 34:1)

> And he wrote on the tablets the words of the covenant—the ten commandments. (Exodus 34:28)

This restoration of the tablets did not incorporate *any* concession to the collective will of the people who had rebelled against the aristocratic-theocratic order. Neither did the renewed covenant now inscribed upon the restored tablets incorporate *any* revision of the original law. Rather, the ten commandments which had been engraved on the original stone tablets were engraved again, unchanged, on the second (restored) tablets.

⊕

In the falling away of the people of Israel during the Sinai revelation, in the subsequent renewal of the covenant with them through the intercession of Moses, and in the ensuing restoration of the stone tablets, we have before us the origin and essence of the archetypal phenomenon of *dogma*. An event of immense significance in cultural history took place when, in the desert of Sinai toward the end of the second millennium before Christ, in a world of myths and their associated cults, the formless and timeless God revealed himself as THE ONE WHO IS. The religions of the surrounding cultures at that time were made up of an aggregation of myths featuring a panoply of mythical figures. But here was no trace of dogma, and thus no obligatory articles of faith. Such mythological traditions remained open to diverse interpretations; they were not considered ends in themselves. Their influence lay in the *suggestive power* of their cultic practices.

Now, what greater difference can be conceived than that between mythological-cultic traditions (open to, even inviting, diverse interpretations) and the *primal dogma* proclaimed at the revelation on Mt. Sinai: "I am the LORD (YHVH), your God . . . you shall have no other gods before me"? For three thousand years this proclamation has been repeated daily by the Jewish faithful in their *Shema,* or declaration of faith:

> Hear, O Israel, the LORD (*Adonai*) our God, the
> LORD is one. (Deut. 6:4)

This proclamation has also been received into the Christian Creed as its first article of faith:

> *Credo in unum Deum, Pat rem omni potentem, factorem*
> *coeli et terrae, visibilium omnium et invisibilium.*
>
> I believe in one God, the Father, the Almighty, maker
> of heaven and earth, and of all that is seen and unseen.

What was new about the primal dogma of monotheism was not that the multiplicity of existence derives from the Oneness of the Being of THE ONE WHO IS, or even that the true God is One, for these truths in themselves were not new, but that they were proclaimed as dogma, as obligatory articles of faith.

It cannot be denied that the truths proclaimed by this primal dogma were known already to the spiritual elite of the mythologizing religions: the "pagan" initiates. At their most accomplished level they, at least, could penetrate the mythic veil and thereby gain entry to the truth of the *one* God. This must be conceded by any who are acquainted with the writings and fragments attributed to Hermes Trismegistus, with those attributed to Pythagoras, or with the writings of Plato and the Stoics. This is true also of the many "esoteric" teachings sprung from the soil of the mythic writings of the Vedas (the Upanishads)—which likewise have, as their principal object, knowledge of the *one* God of the world.

But such insights as we are speaking of were gained by the initiates of the pagan mythologizing religions only at the *conclusion* of a stepwise path leading from the world of *existence* (together with its native forces) to that of *essence*; whereas now, at the revelation on Mt. Sinai, those insights had been proclaimed to a nomadic people *right from the beginning* as an article of faith, a dogma. Whereas the philosophers, adepts, and initiates of the mythologizing pagan religions struggled to attain higher knowledge by the *end* of their initiatic schooling, this same higher knowledge had been proclaimed at the *outset* by Moses in the Sinai desert to a nomadic people lacking any preparatory schooling whatsoever! The "omega" of the experiential path of knowledge practiced in the ancient mysteries had become, for the community of the faithful of Israel, the "alpha" of the Sinai revelation.

⊕

The essence of dogma has nothing to do with an injunction to abandon active thinking and the quest for insight. Dogma is, rather, a gift from heaven that *orients* our active thinking and quest for insight toward divine truth. It is not a prohibition of active thinking and investigation; instead, it is a summons to lead them toward divine truth. Dogma is like a star in the heaven of eternal Being that shines unceasingly and inexhaustibly into the world of temporal existence. Dogma stimulates, impels, and guides us toward a state of sympathetic conviviality that opens up our faculty of insight to *moral logic*, which is the logic of divine wisdom. And because moral logic arises in us through the union (even fusion) of head-thinking and heart-thinking, it is *more* than capable of grasping the truth of dogmas founded on revelation. This is exactly what we are doing when we are able to re-echo with the Logos: "All things were made through Him, and nothing that was made was made without Him." (John 1:3) The logic of the Logos *illumines* dogma, through and through. And in the light of the Logos, dogma radiates with the clarity of the sun.

⊕

Now, the primal dogma proclaimed at the revelation on Mt. Sinai exhibits all the essential prerequisites, conditions, and pitfalls to be expected in the development and proclamation of a dogma. The fundamental prerequisite of dogma is *revelation*, which, as a rule, is then remanifested from time to time in various forms. Now, in terms of content, the Sinai revelation was just such a remanifestation—that of the intimate personal revelation given long before to the patriarchs Abraham, Isaac, and Jacob—but it was also *unique* in having taken place publicly, before the eyes of all the people of Israel. Yes, Moses had also earlier received the revelation intimately in the "burning bush," but the revelation he later received on Mt. Sinai—as a public event directed to *all* the people of Israel—differed from all previous revelations:

> And the Lord said to Moses, "Thus you shall say to
> the Israelites: 'You have seen for yourselves that I
> have talked *with you* from heaven.'" (Exodus 20:22)

This revelation was addressed to the entire new community of faith that was founded by the Sinai revelation. And so the very first of all dogmas was *not* founded on a private revelation but on a revelation intended for an entire community of faith. Here we see already what is essential to *ex cathedra* "dogmatic" pronouncements—namely, revelation directed to the entire community of faith. Also essential is that such dogmas be independent of the collective will of that community. They must not be determined or influenced by popular consensus (*consensus populi*) nor be altered to make them more "acceptable" as a stratagem to win majority approval. And yet that very thing happened when Aaron yielded to the collective will of the Israelite community: the golden calf took the place of the dogma regarding the God of Being. (Let this yielding on the part of Aaron stand as a warning for all future millennia!)

The fabrication of the golden calf was *not* undertaken because the people fell to doubting the veracity of the revelation proclaimed by Moses. No, they fashioned it to render that revelation more *endurable* to themselves, justifying their action along a line of thought like this:

> After all, was it not the procreative power that
> increased Jacob's family in Egypt to a people plentiful
> and strong enough to depart Egypt in defiance of
> Pharaoh? And is not the figure of the bull an expres-
> sion of the procreative power *par excellence*? Further-
> more, did not the God who revealed Himself on Mt.
> Sinai—the very same God who revealed Himself ear-
> lier to Abraham—*also* promise Abraham that *his*
> descendants would be as plentiful as the sand of the
> ocean's shores?

And so for those at the foot of Mt. Sinai, the God who spoke to Moses, whose name is THE ONE WHO IS, was recast as the God of procreation, the God who manifests Himself in the "power" of procreation.

⊕

Despite the people's predilections and preferred interpreta-tion, the God-above-the-self was not to be approached by any other means than by the noetic "language of the self"—that is, through moral logic. This is why His name was not to be spoken (even today the name of God, YHVH, is not spoken, but is replaced by *Adonai*, meaning LORD). Thus did it come to pass that this God YHVH was "miscast" by the people of Israel at the foot of the mountain of revelation as the "golden calf," as the force of sexual procreation exerting its power over the self.

What took place on top of Mt. Sinai, and also at its foot, flashes a warning for all time that interpretation of any dogma founded upon revelation *must* remain subject to the same authority as that which first proclaimed it. Dogma may *not* be given over to the collective ability to imagine it or to the interpretive inclinations of the community of believers, of the people, nor even to its priesthood (Aaron and the Levites, in the case of the Israelite community). It may not be interpreted or re-interpreted in a democratic way; otherwise, a *transcendent* truth will be *immanentized*. When this happens, THE ONE WHO IS ("I am the I am") becomes a "golden calf," a symbol of the procreative power. And in consequence, the Son of God—the eternal Word of the Father—is reduced to a "simple man from Nazareth," serving as no more than a model for the "solution to the social question."

Dogma *must* retain its original revelatory character. It is a summons to the life of the heart (*sursum corda*)—to raising heart, thought, and endeavor to its level. Dogma *must not* be made "tenable" or "palatable" on a human level, to the point of being recast according to quotidian social views and values. Dogma comes from above and calls to those below; it must never happen the other way around. For, if it does, that dogma merely expresses the common denominator of the people's or the theologians' opinions about faith.

⊕

The primal dogma of the Sinai revelation was proclaimed to the people in the *same language* in which it had been imparted to Moses. It was not made known in visions or dreams, or in "obscure riddles" or in images drawn from material existence. It was communicated *directly*, "face to face" (Num. 12:8), by direct speech from self to self—that is, in the language of the self, in the language of Being. It is significant that more than a thousand years later, the *new revelation* of the gospels employed the *same* essentialist language of the self, the "I." The "I am the I am" of the God of Being (THE ONE WHO IS) Who revealed Himself to Moses (Exodus 3:14) was followed in the new revelation, the New Testament, by the "I am" sayings of John's gospel, which reveal Christ as the "I am": "I am the Vine, you are the branches"; "I am the Way, the Truth, and the Life"; I am the Door"; "I am the Bread of Life"; "I am the Good Shepherd"; "I am the Light of the World"; "I am the Resurrection and the Life"; and also, "I and the Father are one."

The words "I am the I am" of the Mosaic revelation are as a seed—which, in due season (as recounted in the New Testament), came to blossom and to fruit. It was truly a festal moment in the spiritual history of humanity when, after having (by his silence) rejected various answers from the people, Jesus put to his narrower circle of disciples the question: "But who do *you* say that *I* am?" to which Peter answered: "You are Christ, the Son of the living God." (Matt. 16:15–16) The new community of faith, the Community of Christ, was founded *at that moment*. The See (Seat) of Peter received thereby, for all time, the task and mission of guardianship over the revelation that comes "not from flesh and blood," but "from the Father in heaven." Peter's answer was neither a collation of the varying opinions offered by the people, nor the outcome of deliberations among the circle of disciples (for the latter remained silent); it was, rather, an insight sparked by Peter, an insight that struck like lightning into the mystery of the *I am*—that is, into the mystery of the very One who had posed the question!

⊕

Just as Moses was recipient, proclaimer, and authoritative interpreter of the Sinai revelation, so also (after the event at Caesarea Philippi we have just spoken of) Peter became recipient, proclaimer, and authoritative interpreter of the teaching of the Church. This is the significance, the task, and the mission of the See of Peter, the highest authority in the Church of the New Covenant.

The Eastern Church, having rejected the authority of the See of Peter in favor of the ecumenical council as the single highest authority of the Church, consequently considered itself bound only by the resolutions of the first seven councils. In view of this split, further development of the Eastern Church became impossible, since according to its own understanding no further ecumenical councils could take place. This is why, as far as teaching and practice are concerned, the Eastern Church came to a standstill at the stage it had reached in the tenth and eleventh centuries. Thus it fell into a vicious circle (*circulus vitiosus*): only a council representing the undivided Church can further deepen and clarify traditional teaching and practice, but such a council presupposes unity between the two Churches—which, however, must be ruled out. This is because the Catholic Church stands by the *papal principle*, to which the Eastern

Church, which stands by the *conciliar principle*, cannot grant recognition.

Owing to this standstill and the resulting divergence and separation, the Eastern Church took no part in the development of the magnificent theological and philosophical edifice of Scholasticism. It was unable to benefit from the cultural and moral fruits matured and ripened in the Western spiritual orders (Benedictines, Carmelites, Dominicans, Franciscans, and Jesuits, to name only the largest ones). Furthermore, since it had no alternative but to relegate standards of canonization to local ethnic and national usage, no universal protocol for this purpose could be established. In the end, the price of falling away from the See of Peter in favor of the conciliar principle was, on the one hand, disintegration into many independent national and regional churches, and on the other, coming to a halt in the development of dogmatic, moral, and exegetical theology. All this followed unavoidably from interpreting Christ's words "You are Peter (*petros*), the rock, and on this rock (*petra*) I will build my Church, and the gates of the realm of death will not overcome it" to mean, rather, "You are the rocks, and on these rocks I will build my Church, and the gates of death will not overcome them."

⊕

The questions detailed above, which proved to be of such vital importance for the Church, had *already* arisen long before; they found their answers in the primal phenomenon of the founding by Moses of the first monotheistic faith through the revelation on Mt. Sinai. Already *then*, the problem of authority had been raised: whether it comes from below and represents nothing more than the will of

34

the people, or whether it is tied to an office bestowed from above (howsoever the individual occupant of this office may be determined). And the decision made was in favor of the office. In the cultural circumstances prevailing at that time, the problem presented itself as one between revealed dogma (articles of faith obligatory for all) on the one hand, and the capacity and intellectual inclination (or lack thereof) of the people of the faith community to comprehend it on the other—that is, whether it is permissible to *adapt* revealed dogma to the demands of the majority of the faithful. And the decision rendered was in favor of the *invariability* of dogma. In those long-ago days, the question "rule of the people or of the hierarchical order?" was decided clearly in favor of the latter. The events on Mt. Sinai are the very archetype and model of hierarchical order. From the top of the mountain rang out the voice of God, THE ONE WHO IS, proclaiming to His chosen one, Moses, the infallible commandments—while at the mountain's foot, the people worshipped as "their" god a creation of their own willful devising.

THE
SECOND
COMMANDMENT

"You Shall Not Make For Yourself A Graven Image"

Law Against Forming an Image or Likeness as a Precondition for Revelation and Knowledge of Being

"You shall not make for yourself an image in the form of anything in heaven above or on the earth beneath or in the waters below. You shall not bow down to them or worship them; for I, the LORD your God, am a jealous God, punishing the children of Israel for the sin of the parents to the third and fourth generation of those who hate me, but showing love to a thousand generations of those who love me and keep my commandments."   Exodus 20:4–6

HE INTRODUCTORY PRAYER OF THE MASS OF ST. Pope Pius V contains the following text from the forty-third psalm (third verse):

Emitte lucem tuam et veritatem tuam; ipsa me deduxerunt et adduxerunt in montem sanctum tuum, et in tabernacula tua.

> Send forth your light and your truth; they will serve
> as my guide. Let them bring me to your holy moun-
> tain, to the place of your dwelling.

As is the case with many of the psalms, this prayer contains indications about essential facts of spiritual life and mystical experience as they relate to two paths: the path of light (or day) and the path of darkness (or night). In theology one speaks (as regards these two paths) of *positive* theology, for example that of Thomas Aquinas, and of *negative* theology, for example that of Dionysius the Areopagite, the so-called pseudo-Dionysius.[1]

Positive theology proceeds from the supposition that intensifying and elevating our capacity for conceptualization *along the path of analogy* engenders conceptions that approach as nearly as possible to the Being of God, which in itself is beyond conception. Negative theology, by contrast, proceeds from the supposition that our capacity for conceptualization is fundamentally incapable of grasping the Being of God. Thus, for negative theology, every idea, however lofty and spiritual it may be, nevertheless is and remains a mental picture that intrudes between or "distances" the conceptualizing individual from the Being of God, covering over or obscuring the *reality* of His Nature.

The path of negative theology leads to *mysticism*: the real, living experience of the revelation of the Being of God in

---

[1] Concerning the controversy regarding the person of Dionysius, Monsignor Darboy, the archbishop of Paris, makes a convincing case for the authenticity of the writings ascribed to him. See his introduction to the collected works of Dionysius, translated by Darboy from Greek into French in 1932. AUTHOR

the soul. The path of positive theology, by contrast, leads to *analogical knowledge* of God through symbol or likeness—that is, to grasping His Nature metaphorically through the refinement and elevation of mental pictures and concepts. This is the path of the progressive *approach* of human reason and conceptual power to the Being of God.

Ultimately, these two paths derive from a difference in psycho-spiritual predisposition determined by destiny. Some cannot do otherwise than see in Creation the revelation of the work of the Creator, which proclaims Him and is no other than His image and likeness—as in the hymn: "Heaven and earth are filled with your glory" (*Pleni sunt coeli et terra gloria tua*). Others are fated to yearn in silent darkness for the revelation of the Being of God. In other words, there are *day souls*, those who in the light of day experience the visible and invisible things and beings of the world as revelations of God; and there are *night souls*, those who in the unlit and unsounding depths of Being—where there is no other light than that of conscience and no other voice than that of conscience—sense the reality of the Being of God. The Franciscan St. Bonaventure and the Carmelite St. John of the Cross serve well as representatives of these two orientations.

⊕

To St. Bonaventure, the world of visible and invisible things and creatures was

> *Si patet quod totus mundus est sicut unum speculum plenum luminibus prac sentantibus divinam sapientiam et sicut carbo effundens lucem.*[2]

[2] II *Sententiae* 9.

a mirror full of lights, representing divine wisdom,
and like burning coals radiating out light.

For him, the world was "the other Holy Scripture"; its
beings and facts were the symbols that reveal God, just as
the words of the Bible do. And just as Holy Scripture has a
literal meaning, which is historical and factual, so too does
the Book of Creation—which is the world—initially have a
"literal" meaning. But behind this more superficially "literal" meaning of the word (just as in the case of Holy Scripture) lies hidden a deeper moral, theological, and mystical
meaning. Thus, just as penetrating insight, the capacity to
see clearly into the heart of the matter, makes it possible to
pass beyond the literal meaning of Holy Scripture to its
moral, theological, and mystical sense, so also is there a way
of experiencing the world and life—a *beholding* through
the light of the Logos "that is the light of humanity"—that
transforms experience of the Creation into a revelation of
the Creator behind it. Such a beholding transforms whoever participates in it into a *seer* who apprehends not only
the world of the senses but also the suprasensible world—
i.e., the world of souls and of the angelic hierarchies—
which is more resplendent with light than is the world of
the senses and bears more immediate witness to God. The
world of the senses (the kingdoms of nature) *testifies* to the
all-prevailing wisdom of God, whereas the world of the
soul (the angelic world) *represents* this wisdom, in that it
lives from and in this wisdom. St. Bonaventure's message
was that the world of visible and invisible things can be
seen *in* and *through* the divine light, and that this kind of
clear seeing strengthens, confirms, and deepens the truth of
revelation. Such experience of the world in the light of
grace is a support for faith.

40

⊕

The path and the experience of St. John of the Cross, author of *The Night of the Senses and the Night of the Spirit*, are different. John of the Cross renounced "experience of the day-lit world" and strove instead for the experience—emptied of images and analogical reasonings—of meeting God in the darkness of the senses and of the mind. For him, the mirroring of God in the world was unimportant, as were also the mental images and analogies or metaphors which ordinary experience affords to support and confirm faith. What was important for him was the encounter of the *being* of the soul with the *Being* of God, with the *Reality* of God Himself, with the *Truth* of God. But this encounter is not possible by any accustomed manner of beholding or knowing; it can only happen through the reciprocal embrace of God's Love and the soul's love. And this in turn can only happen in the complete absence of perceptual images and mental analogies—that is, in the "night of the spirit."

Now, this night of the spirit in which the most immediate imaginable experience of the loving embrace of the soul by the Being of God can take place is not in fact darkness, but "absolute light"; it is the light that "blinds" because of its superabundance, and is therefore experienced as darkness. This absolute light, experienced as darkness, is the *radiance* of the reality of God; it is the truth of God, which permeates and envelops the soul.

⊕

Let us turn again to the forty-second psalm:

Emitte lucem tuam et veritatem tuam: ipsa me deduxerunt et adduxerunt in montem sanctum tuum, et in tabernacula tua.

Paraphrasing, this means to say:

> Let me experience life and the world in your light;
> envelop and permeate me with the darkness of the
> direct revelation of your essence, your reality, the
> truth of your Being itself. For, experience of the
> world and of life in your light, and in the truth of your
> Being, will lead me out of the narrowness of my self.
> It will grant me the all-encompassing view, from on
> high, of the world of experience ("bring me to your
> holy mountain") while translating me into your inner
> presence and union with you (*tabernacula tua,* your
> "dwelling").

The holy mountain and the dwelling (or tabernacle) of
God are the twin goals of the two paths—the path of light
and day, and the path of darkness and night—as represented by St. Bonaventure and St. John of the Cross. The
goal of Bonaventure is *ascent*: elevation of the spirit to
behold the world in divine light, so that it appears as the
revelation of God. The goal of John of the Cross is *descent*:
into the depths of the human soul, where the aspirant
encounters the Being of God directly, and where they
embrace one another. Beholding the world as revelation in
the light of God is the condition of the soul "on the holy
mountain"; the intimate inner experience of God indwell-
ing the soul is the condition of the soul "in the dwelling of
God." In the forty-third psalm these two conditions are
called the *light of God* and the *truth of God*. We may, then,
also call the night path the path of "truth."

Now, according to its spirit as well as to its text, the Sinai
revelation expressly emphasizes the "truth" of God—that is,
the quality of God (of which neither image nor likeness can

42

be made)[3] encountered on the path to experiencing Him in the nocturnal darkness of the spirit. This is clear not only from the words:

> You shall not make for yourself a graven image, or
> any likeness of anything that is in heaven above or on
> the earth below, or that is in the water under the earth.
> (Exodus 20:4)

It is clear also from the "prophetic" nature of Moses as we find it described in the twelfth chapter of the book of Numbers, where we read:

> Hear my words: if there is a prophet among you, I the
> LORD make myself known to him in a vision, I speak
> with him in a dream. Not so with my servant Moses;
> he is entrusted with all my house. With him I speak
> mouth to mouth, clearly and not in riddles; indeed, he
> beholds the form of the LORD. (Numbers 12:6–8)

In other words, THE ONE WHO IS revealed Himself directly to Moses in the clear light of day consciousness, and *without* recourse to symbolic dreams and visions. He spoke with Moses directly, revealing Himself to Moses as He *is* (in "His form," as Luther translates it). This means, however, that regarding the two paths characterized above as the day path and the night path—or the path of light and the path of truth—God's revelation to Moses took place on the path of truth.[4] This is also confirmed in the book of Deuteronomy, where we read concerning Moses:

---

[3] *Bildlose Unvorstellbarkeit.*
[4] Even though received in the clear light of day.

> Never since has there arisen a prophet since in Israel like Moses, whom the LORD knew face to face. (Deut. 34:10)

This knowing was reciprocal ("face to face"): it was a direct approach of God to the human being and of the human being to God, a mutual permeation. That is why both declarations could be made in the Bible—namely, that in contrast to other prophets, Moses knew God directly (Num. 12:6–8), and that he was known by God like no other prophet. (Deut. 34:10) The two declarations represent a *single* process of reciprocal approach. Taken together, they signify the disappearance of any possible distance between God and Moses, even such scant distance as "seeing or beholding in the light" might presuppose. In the case of Moses, what is present is actually the revelation of God in "His truth," and not the revelation in "His light": that is, God's revelation in the sense of the night path of St. John of the Cross, not in the sense of the day path of St. Bonaventure. Furthermore, as we shall shortly see, the night path turns out to be also the path of *life after death*:

> Now I know only in part; then I will know fully, even as I have been fully known. (1 Cor 13:12)

⊕

Now, everything indicates that the path taken by the Israelite community of faith was fundamentally the same path that Moses took, for both his destiny and the destiny of Israel were determined by a wandering in the desert: it was a *desert path*. Just as Moses had to go to Mt. Horeb in the desert, where he was to experience the first revelation of THE ONE WHO IS ("I am the I am"), so did the people of Israel also have to go up out of Egypt into the desert, where they were to experience the revelation on Mt. Sinai and become the community of faith of Israel. It was in the desert that Moses experienced the first revelation of God in the burning bush, and it was again in the desert that the community of Israel experienced the revelation on Mt. Sinai. Furthermore, it was only after wandering in the desert for forty years that the people of Israel were allowed to enter the promised land. Moses, however, did not cross the Jordan into the promised land. Instead, he crossed to the far side of the threshold of death—to his "promised land."

⊕

Yes, the people of Israel prepared themselves for their future encounter with the awaited Messiah in the promised land, but it was granted Moses to experience this encounter with the Messiah after crossing the threshold of death—that is, in the disembodied state. This encounter took place in the company of Elijah at the scene of the Transfiguration on Mt. Tabor. Peter, James, and John witnessed this encounter: not only the meeting of Moses and Elijah with Christ but also the conversation Christ entered into with the two prophets.

Moses and Elijah were not hindered by death from meeting the living Messiah now come down to earth. They spoke with the Living One, as did other Israelites who had occasion to do so at that time. It was as "living ones" that Moses and Elijah were granted the occasion to converse with *the* Living One. So great was the impression made by Moses and Elijah as "living ones" upon Peter, James, and John, that the three immediately suggested raising up three tabernacles (dwellings) on the heights of Mt. Tabor: "one for Jesus, one for Elijah, and one for Moses." (Matt. 17:4)

On that occasion Moses and Elijah seemed just as alive as was Jesus.

The desert wandering of the people of Israel under the leadership of Moses had a greater significance, however, than that of just any migration of a nomadic people. Their wandering arose, not out of the accustomed pattern of nomadic life, but from an inner necessity associated with the path of *withdrawal* and *purification*. Egypt, along with all its cities, buildings, temples, and cultic celebrations had to be left behind, put out of the Israelites' mind, so that they might be purged of its influence. The path through the desert was a schooling, an inner preparation for the revelation-to-come, a revelation whose precondition was a state of soul emptied of memories, images, and reasonings. Just as a glass can be refilled only after being emptied, so can a soul receive a new revelation only if first emptied. The Israelite people's wandering in the desert under the leadership of Moses was just such an emptying in preparation for being filled with a new revelation. The goal of this pilgrimage was surely not to reach the promised land of Canaan: two weeks would have sufficed to travel from the eastern boundary of Egypt to Canaan! The forty years' wandering was unrelated to the geographical distance to the final destination: it was, rather, an end in itself.

The loneliness of the desert would in the end prove to be the decisive, guiding experience for the whole future spiritual path of the chosen people. For the twelve tribes of Israel were chosen as representatives of humanity to set an example by walking the desert path, that is, by undertaking to experience the pure revelation of God "without image or likeness." They were chosen to lead humanity by example on the path to pure intuition—that is, to knowledge of God independent of mental representation of any kind.

The path of "inner certainty" that we are speaking of is founded upon *nothing*. It is the path of pure *belief* in the sense of Christ's words:

> Have you believed because you have seen me?
> Blessed are those who *have not seen* and yet believe.
> (John 20:29)

This capacity for belief was prepared by the desert wandering of the twelve tribes of Israel with Moses. Their journey through the desert taught them that giving up both image and likeness as agencies of mental representation constitutes *the* essential precondition both for the *revelation* of God and for *knowledge* of His Being.

⊕

St. John of the Cross likens those who walk the desert path (or night path) to adults who require no outside support, who need not be carried as they go their way. Such adults forego the consolations of the dreams, visions, and sunny moods accorded the nurturing embrace of childhood. Adults endure the inevitable tedium and unpleasantries of living out of their own inner resources, whereas the child has need still of entertainment, comfort, and encouragement. For this reason, St. John of the Cross knew his way of purification through the inner desert to be a path only for mature souls—souls robust enough to bear the tedium, stillness, and loneliness of the night of the spirit.

But even such souls do still have need of being strengthened, uplifted, and encouraged! It is one of the experiences of those walking the desert path that at night, when asleep, something ever and again refreshes their strength to endure and not despair. Over time, the night—which can at first seem just as desert-like, unmoving, and dark as does the night of the spirit to the waking consciousness of day—transforms itself into a bestower of *strength of soul* and *courage of spirit*. It is as though something received during the night, like an after-echo from the heavenly choirs, grants new life and strength to the soul (and often to the body also) of the desert wanderer as he awakens, bringing with it renewed courage for life and the temporary dispersal of any sense of hopelessness. This strengthening is not owing to a dream or to any kind of instruction received while dreaming, but purely and simply to the *condition* of the soul which prevails during the night. Despondency or despair simply disappear of their own accord. One is reinvigorated and continues down the desert path with renewed vitality.

It would not be in the least arbitrary to compare the after-echo of the night of which we are speaking with the miraculous nourishment of *manna* that was provided to the chosen people during their desert wanderings. For the experience of nocturnal strengthening must be lived *anew* each night; it cannot be stored up for the following days as a content of memory. In the sunlight of day consciousness the strengthening night experience "melts away." It loses its potency.

The analogy between the experience of the refreshing effect or "feeding" during sleep (known to those who "wander in the desert"), and the feeding with divine *manna* of which the Bible tells, goes further—extending even to taste and color. In the Bible, *manna* is called the bread of heaven or the bread of the angels (Psalms 78:23–25), which, like dew or frost, covered the immediate area around the Israelites' camp each morning. Consisting of seeds the size and shape of coriander, it was white, and tasted like honey-cake. (Exodus 16:31) Now, the strengthening night-effect that the "spiritual" desert wanderer can receive is also experienced as white and is perceived as sweet (as in the expression "sleeping sweetly"). White and sweet is the overall impression experienced upon awakening; but in fact, the experience results from the integration of countless, tiny, uniform entities, somewhat in the sense of the *petites perceptions* (minute impressions) of the philosopher and mathematician Leibniz.[5] In what by analogy with "physics" might be called "pneumatics," these tiny impressions play a role analogous to that of the smallest physical particles (*corpuscula*), which, though invisible on account of their minuteness (and for that reason unnoticed), can nevertheless wield great significance and influence. Upon awakening, the totality of these tiny impressions does in fact leave behind the overall impression of whiteness and sweetness; and their uniform multiplicity make well for a comparison with coriander seeds. (Exodus 16:31) Also, their combined effect is strengthening; it is refreshing and nourishing. Thanks to this effect, the strength of the desert wanderer is restored sufficiently to take up again and continue further on the desert path, with all its monotony and sparse stimulation—wandering "without image or likeness," without dreams and visions.

It must be emphasized that we are speaking here of the *analogy* between the strengthening after-echo of sleep (as this can be experienced by those such as St. John of the Cross, who travel the desert path) and the *manna* of the biblical account. Here it is not a matter of *identity* in con-

---

[5] Leibniz, *Nouveaux Essais sur l'entendement humain*, III, 1.

sidering the concrete reality of this biblical miracle. It is true that biblical miracles are not to be understood merely as symbolic pictures representing psychological and spiritual experiences; but on the other hand it would be a mistake to consider *manna* as signifying nothing more than the sugary substance that lice living on the tamarisks of the Sinai peninsula secrete as fine grains!

The analogy we are referring to opens up the possibility of contemplating the moral-spiritual dimension of "heavenly sustenance." This is not simply something to marvel at, but something to understand. To understand something by its analogical relationship with a reality in the moral and psychological domain does not however preclude the possibility of this something also playing a role as a concrete event in outer, historical reality. The Bible does not speak only in symbols or only of facts: it speaks of facts that are at the same time symbols. Thus, for the chosen people, their wandering in the desert for forty years under the leadership of Moses was *factual*, but it was at the same time *symbolic* as signifying preparation for the revelation of the God of whom no image or likeness can be made. That is, it prepared the people of Israel for the revelation of God in His Truth and Reality.

As a *fact*, the wandering in the desert was an historical occurrence; as a *symbol*, it is an expression of the timeless law of the necessity of purification and "emptied consciousness" as precondition for the revelation of God in His truth. This is the same truth expressed in the Sermon on the Mount in the Beatitude:

> Blessed are the poor in spirit, for theirs is the kingdom of heaven. (Matt. 5:3)

THE
THIRD
COMMANDMENT

"You Shall Not Take the Name
of the Lord Your God in Vain"

The Unutterable Name of God

"You shall not misuse the name of the LORD your
God, for the LORD will not hold anyone guiltless
who misuses his name."   Exodus 20:7

N THE "DEPTH LANGUAGE" OF MORAL LOGIC—
that is, in the language of the Old and New Test-
aments—words, concepts, and ideas having to
do with names, giving names, naming, and calling by a name carry a far deeper meaning as regards knowledge of beings, and of their activity, than ordinary language
can give them. By contrast, the superficial, so-called trans-
parently clear, intellectual language of today most often
refers only to *appearances* and fails to penetrate the *essence* of
things. In this connection, let us consider the following passage in the Bible:

> And out of the ground, the LORD God (*Elohim*)
> formed every beast of the field and every bird of the
> air; and He brought them to Adam to see what he

51

would name them; and whatever Adam called every
living creature, that was its name. (Genesis 2:19)

This does not mean that the man Adam coined names for
the beings of the animal kingdom, and even less that he
classified them according to genera and species along the
lines of the Linnaean system, but that he received and fulfilled the divine mandate to determine the functions or missions (relative to man) of the living creatures hierarchically
subordinate to him. For in the language of the Bible, *name*
means "mission" or "essential function"; and *naming* is the
magical act whereby the function or mission of a being is
determined. The new name given by God to Abram
("exalted father"), namely Abraham ("father of a multitude"), is understandable only in this way. For, as we read:

> No longer shall your name be Abram, but your name
> shall be Abraham; for I have made you the father of a
> multitude of nations. (Genesis 17:5)

How we use, or misuse, a name is a serious matter when we
consider that animal names were given, according to God's
mandate, by the prelapsarian man Adam. And this is all the
more true of the names given by God to men, names like
Abraham (as we have said) or like John, proclaimed by the
Archangel Gabriel to John the Baptist's father Zacharias
when he was serving as priest in the temple (Luke 1:13); and
likewise the name Jesus, which the same archangel proclaimed to the Virgin. (Luke 1:31) Yes, but how is it then
with the name of God—the name whose misuse is
expressly forbidden in the ten commandments?

> You shall not make wrongful use of the name of the
> LORD your God (*Eloheha*), for the LORD (YHWH)

will not hold him guiltless who takes his name in vain.
(Exodus 20:7)

Who can give to the highest of all beings His actual and
effective name? Only God Himself! *Revelation* is the only
possible way of knowing the name of God. Only God can
reveal His name. His name is the name He gives Himself.
No man, not even the wisest, can name God (in the biblical
sense) in such a way that the name would not merely be a
useful designation, but real and effective. That this can be
done by no human being is clear for the reasons to follow.

⊕

Just as we have in our language a name, a word, and a concept ("I") that makes sense *only* when used by the speaker
of himself, and would be senseless if used by another in reference to "me," so is this true also of the name of the God-
above-the-I.[1] The God-above-the-I is like a sun whose separate rays are the I's of individuals. In the words of St.
Augustine, "He is more I myself than I myself am." Now, if
the name "I" is misused if not used by the speaker only of
himself, how much the greater is the misuse when the
name of the God-above-the-I is used of God by someone
other than Him!

Neither is God, for man, a He, a You, or an It. God is
not a being standing in an external relationship to the I of
any man—any more than the I of any man could be God's
own I. Just as a separate ray of eternal Being cannot, in reality, identify itself with the eternal Being from Whom it

---

[1] *Des überichlichen Gottes*: literally, "of the God above the I." Here the
English word "self" is most often used in place of the word "I"—though,
according to the sense of the passage, not always.

radiates, so also an individual human I cannot identify itself with the ultimate source of its own being.

Yet even so, the individual I ought not to view the source of its being as something foreign, as something existing entirely outside its I-nature. For although a solar ray is not the same as the sun that radiates it, nevertheless it is sunlike through and through. In the same way, man's own I-being cannot experience itself otherwise than as an inward radiation of the sun of eternal Being into the realm of temporal existence. To be permitted to utter the name of God in the biblical sense (that is, to do so truly and effectively, without misusing it), man would have to be in the position to speak it in the same way he would speak the word "I" of himself. But *in addition*, he would have to speak it in such a way that, in doing so, the primal source and archetype of Self-hood or I-Nature, of interiorized participation in Being, is implicitly intended and invoked. This is why Judaism *prohibits* uttering the actual and effective name of God. It is also why no man, not even Moses, could ever have invented or given this name. Rather, this name was *revealed* to Moses by God Himself, as is clearly expressed in the text concerning the summons of Moses at Mt. Horeb (Exodus 3:13–15):

> Then Moses said to God: "If when I come to the people of Israel and say to them, 'The God of your fathers has sent me to you,' and they ask me, 'What is His name?' What shall I say to them?" God said to Moses: "I AM THE I AM (EHIYEH ASHER EHIYEH, אהיה אשר אהיה)." And He spoke further: "Say this to the people of Israel, 'I AM (EHIYEH, אהיה) has sent me to you.'"
>
> God (Elohim, אלהים) spoke further to Moses: "Say this to the people of Israel, 'The LORD (YHVH,

יהוה), the God (Elohim) of your fathers, the God of
Abraham, the God of Isaac, and the God of Jacob, has
sent me to you. This is My name forever, and thus I
am to be remembered throughout all generations.'"

The name of God revealed to Moses corresponds to the
Being of God-above-the-I (the divine "I"). The name "I am
the I am" is not the name Moses gave to God, but the name
given and revealed *to* Moses *by* God. It is, then, a name of
such kind that it cannot be used in the sense of "He" or
"It," but only in the sense of *trans-subjective* Being. The
name of God is not related by analogy, by likeness, by picture, or by image with any aspect of existence other than
the "I am" experience of man. The most intuitive, intimate
experience of man, the "I am," is the *only* "image and likeness" it contains.

⊕

In fact, *two* names of God were revealed to Moses: one
name that is, so to speak, *absolute*: "I am the I am" or "I am";
and a second name, YHVH, "He is," the name of the God of
Abraham, Isaac, and Jacob, which "to His remembrance" is
to remain valid throughout all generations. To Moses, then,
was revealed both the timeless, absolute, cosmic name "I
am," and the name valid for historical time, the name of the
"God of the fathers," YHVH (YAHVEH).

EHIYEH ("I am") is the name for the realm of *eternal*
Essence or Being. YHVH ("He is") is the name meant for
the realm of *temporal* history, the realm of Existence.[2]
(YHVH, as is now generally recognized, is pronounced

___

[2] That is, Being (*Sein*) and Existence (*Dasein*, lit. "being there").

"Yahveh," not "Yehovah,"[3] which came into use through a misreading.)

YAHVEH is the name for the "above" partner in the covenanted pair Israel–YAHVEH. It contains, and also reveals, the meaning and nature of the divinely-willed mission of Israel as the chosen people, who are in fact known historically as the "people of YAHVEH." The tetragrammaton (YHVH), the "name composed of four letters," contains the secret of fatherhood, motherhood, childhood, and family. The four letters (Yod-Hé-Vau-Hé) stand for this fourfoldness: *Yod* for the eternal masculine, the eternally active and creative; the first *Hé* for the eternal feminine, the receiving and nurturing; *Vau* for the eternal child, ever born and reborn; the second *Hé* for the family, as its principle and archetype.

> Therewith is the name EHIYEH (אהיה) the name
> God gives Himself in the first person; it relates to the
> *subjective* aspect of divine Being. And the name Yod-
> Hé-Vau-Hé (יהוה), given in the third person, relates
> to its *objective* aspect that was revealed to the people
> of Israel.

Thus writes Francis Warrain on the subject of the two names in his work, *La Théodicée de la Kabbale*, the deepest, most comprehensive investigation available of the teachings of the Kabbalah concerning the names of God and the system of the ten *sephiroth* (see below).

According to Jean de Pauly (translator of the *Zohar* into French, and an expert on the text also), the name EHIYEH indicates God's dominion in *heaven*, and the name YHVH

---

[3] In English, usually "Jehovah."

His sovereign power on *earth*. In other words, the name EHIYEH ("I am") is the name of God in heaven, in the realm of eternal Being; the name YHVH ("He is") relates to material existence, the realm of Becoming—the world of earthly and historical events. YHVH is the name for the "God of the fathers." Thus, YHVH is also the holy ensign of the providential covenant underlying the mission of the descendants of Abraham, Isaac, and Jacob to become and to endure as the people of YAHVEH until the culmination of that covenant with the appearance of the Messiah.

⊕

In Hebrew, the names of God EHIYEH ("I am") and YHVH ("He is") are both forms of the verb "to be." In fact, they are in the verb's *future tense*; but in Hebrew this tense signifies not only the future but (and much more so) *duration, permanence.* EHIYEH is conjugated in the first person future durative, whereas the temporal indicator of YHVH is evident in the expression "He is, He was, and He will be."

The name "I am" (EHIYEH) was unutterable because none could legitimately speak it. It was only ever spoken once—by Jesus in answer to the ironic question of the Jews, as reported in John's gospel:

> "You are not yet fifty years old and have seen Abra-
> ham?" Jesus said to them: "Truly, truly, I say to you,
> before Abraham was, I am." So they took up stones
> to throw at him; but Jesus hid himself, and went out
> of the temple. (John 8:57–59)

As regards the second name, "He is" or the ONE-WHO-IS (YHVH), only the high priest was allowed to reverently voice it, and even then, only once a year at a celebration in the Holy of Holies in the Temple. Otherwise the name ADONAI (LORD) was used in place of the unutterable name, as also when reading the Holy Scriptures. Only on this one occasion, when the high priest reverently spoke it, could the name YHVH be spoken without its utterance constituting a misuse of God's name. For in the cultural outlook of the world of the Bible, to *speak* a name meant to release its *summoning* power. Uttering a name was tantamount to a magical invocation. And therein lies the risk of egregiously misusing the holy name. This explains how Martin Buber came to the view that the revelation of the name YHVH in the third chapter of Exodus illustrates above all that there was no need to summon the LORD by name, for in fact He was always already present with His power and help. Buber therefore translates the name YHVH as "I am there"—for, after all, the Ever-Present One need not be summoned!

> YHVH, the God of your fathers, the God of Abraham, the God of Isaac, and the God of Jacob, has sent me to you. This is My name forever, and thus I am to be remembered throughout all generations.

This was the mandate given Moses concerning the name YHVH. It was *not* said that "with this name I am to be *summoned* throughout all generations," but that "with this name I am to be *remembered* throughout all generations." YHVH is, so to say, the name of God for inner, meditative use, and not for outward utterance or any kind of magical invocation.

But even inner, meditative use of the name of the "God of the fathers and their descendants throughout all generations" is liable to misuse, and this is a particularly present danger once the secret of the name has been recognized. What is this secret? It is no other than the historical mission of the people of Israel! What, then, is the significance of this historical mission?

⊕

The name YHVH bears within it the divinely-willed mission (through the powers of procreation and heredity) to create and preserve a people set apart, a people that finds itself a stranger to the inhabitants of other lands, often even fundamentally at odds with them. For this people set apart is destined to be the keeper of a living tradition (borne by heredity) of the covenant with YHVH—ever nurturing the hope that, through this covenant, redemption from the consequences of the Fall will in due season follow. The significance of procreation and heredity for this mission is clearly evident in the text of the Decalogue concerning the nature of YHVH's justice and mercy:

> For I, the LORD (YHVH), your God, am a jealous
> God, visiting the iniquity of the fathers upon the chil-
> dren to the third and the fourth generation of those
> who hate me, but showing mercy to a thousand gen-
> erations of those who love me and keep my com-
> mandments. (Exodus 20:5–6)

There is no mention in this passage of single souls, of individualities. It is, rather, a matter of justice and mercy for the generations of the hereditary stream.

Now, such an understanding of justice and mercy stands in stark contrast to that prevalent in India and Tibet (and increasingly now in Europe and America) as the *law of karma*, which is by contrast oriented to *individuals* and not to generations of descendants. The idea of karma is founded on the proposition: "What *you* sow, *you* will reap." Each of us will bear the consequences of what we set in motion by our actions. Others will not bear those consequences—least of all our descendants!

Quite evidently, then, even though the law of punishment for sins and reward for righteousness as proclaimed in the Decalogue is a moral law, it nonetheless works through heredity and procreation. In the case of the people set apart, it is thus the *bloodline* that actually bears both the curse of sin and the blessing of righteousness through the generations.

In short, the name of the "God of the fathers" with which one is to remember for all time the God of Israel who led the people of Israel out of Egypt (that is, the name YHVH), reveals and contains the moral law of retribution and selection holding sway over procreation and heredity through the generations. This law was proclaimed and expressly intended for the chosen people, for they were the ones set apart to fulfill the mission of preparing for the coming of the Redeemer of all humankind. Put another way, the coming of the Redeemer is the final cause (*causa finalis*) of the existence and destiny of that people. The Redeemer is the very *raison d'être* for the choosing of this people! In truth, the name YHVH signifies, historically, the sanctification of procreation and heredity: procreation and heredity are made sacred through this name.

Insight into this special relationship of YHVH to procreation and heredity can, however, as we have mentioned before, lead to misuse of the holy name of God: from the one side by using it to summon Him through magical invocation; from the other by failing to grasp that the force of procreation and heredity is no more than a *reflection* of the name (by which we mean the divinely-willed mission of Israel), and thus mistaking that force for the name itself. In the latter case, the God of Israel is falsely seen as a kind of religious infrastructure built up from the forces of procreation and heredity—instead of being seen "through" the procreative forces as in fact constituting their divine archetype. But in this way, the *merely* procreative is projected upon the divine archetype. Now, such a projection amounts in essence to the same thing (and thereby revisits or repeats) what took place at the foot of Mt. Sinai, when it was the "procreative" golden calf—and not God's name—that was worshipped as divine. Indeed, the people at the foot of the mountain even elevated the procreative power to the rank of the "God who led us out of Egypt"!

To let this mistaken understanding stand, to leave this misuse of the divine name unchallenged and uncorrected, would amount to a kind of "Freudian" misinterpretation of the religion and the mission of YHVH. Set alongside the other misuse of God's name (seeking to summon YHVH through magical invocation), we see just how grave this misuse of His name is. But as is written:

> The LORD (YHVH) will not allow to go unpunished whoever misuses his name. (Exodus 20:7)

INTERLUDE

The Use of God's
Name in Meditation

E HAVE SEEN THAT TWO NAMES WERE REVEALED to Moses on Mt. Horeb: "I am" (EHIYEH, אהיה), and "He is" or "He Who is Being" (YHVH, יהוה). The first name refers to atemporal existence, the second to temporal existence—i.e., in our present case, to the historical mission of the people of Israel. The second name designates the God of Abraham, Isaac, and Jacob; the first name designates the God who says of Himself "Before Abraham was, *I am*," as is stated in John's gospel (i.e., He who is atemporal and, as such, not limited to one people and to that people's temporal, historical mission). The name "I am Who I am" is the answer to the question of humanity, whose representative Moses was. More exactly, it was the answer directed to Moses as that representative—and it was meant for *him*. By contrast, the name YHVH was the answer meant for the Israelite *people*. For Moses, who was summoned with this latter name by the "angel of the LORD" from the burning bush, received the revelation (which then followed) both as the representative of humanity and as the individual given the task of creating a *new people* from the descendants of the three patriarchs, and of leading them out of Egypt.

The exodus from Egypt was the birth of the people of

Israel. This people consisted of the descendants of the sons of Jacob and of other slaves of the state of Egypt who joined them and departed with them. The people led by Moses into the desert represented a vibrant mix of familial and tribal traditions. Furthermore, the divine revelation that had been imparted to the patriarchs was not identical to what Moses received at the foot of Mt. Horeb, for God did *not* reveal Himself to the patriarchs as YHVH, let alone as "I am" (EHIYEH), but as SHADDAI (שרי), the "Almighty One." This name corresponded to the stage at which God was manifested and understood at that time. The name SHADDAI was used when it was a matter of impressing upon humanity that, for God, nothing is impossible (Gen. 17:1; 28:3; 35:11; 43:14; 48:3; 49:25). It was with this name that God revealed Himself to Abraham, Isaac, and Jacob. Furthermore, in the account concerning Jacob (Gen. 31:13; 33:20; 35:1; 46:3), God's name EL (לא) is used, meaning the "Strong, the Exalted, the Superior One."

Names of God: Stages of Interiorization

The names of God used in the Bible represent stages in the progressive revelation of the Being of God, stages matched to humanity's developing power of understanding. More particularly, they mark degrees of the increasing interiorization of man's power of understanding, as well as the progressive revelation of aspects of God's Being—again in the direction of interiorization.

SHADDAI: On the path of interiorization we may say that the name SHADDAI ("Almighty One") corresponds to the first, or lowest, stage of understanding God—which goes no further than the morally neutral notion of might or omnipotence. If we compare this level of understanding God with the words of the old Russian prince Alexander Nevski, "God is not in might, but in truth and righteousness" (*Ne w sile Bog a w prawd*), we see how great a step in the interiorization of knowledge of the Being of God this interpretation of St. Alexander Nevski represents. In this connection it must also be mentioned that Adolf Hitler, one of the most amoral and barbarous men of recent time, often expressly appealed to the "Almighty One."

We should note here as well, however, that Moses, to whom the name EHIYEH—the highest of the names of God—was revealed, had nevertheless, in his role as mediator with the Egyptians, to serve the stage of God's revelation corresponding to the name SHADDAI. He did this initially in the magical struggle of rods and snakes, then in the sending of the ten plagues, and finally in the destruction of the Egyptian army in the Red Sea. All these events were revelations of God under the name SHADDAI ("Almighty One"), for it was needful that Pharaoh and the Egyptian people learn what it meant to oppose the will of the Almighty One. And their suffering at the hand of these revelations of power did indeed impress upon them that the God SHADDAI was on the side of the Israelites.

EL: The name EL ("Strong," "Exalted," "Superior One") represents a further stage in the interiorization of knowledge of the Being of God, for here it is not a matter of straightforward might or omnipotence, but of more elevated hierarchical rank, of God's exaltedness in comparison to the human condition. The name EL forms the *beginning* syllable of several other names that express exaltedness, for example EL-HAIA, the "Living God." It also forms the *ending* syllable of various angelic names, as for example Micha*el,* Gabri*el,* Rapha*el,* Uri*el.* EL expresses the attribute of "looking up," of worshipping what is more elevated in the hierarchical order of Being; it presupposes a feeling of reverence and dignity in the hierarchical sense, a feeling for the divinity of God's Being. By this we mean more than merely "acknowledging" a power superior to that of man. Reverence signifies a more *interior* relationship to God than that of fear before the power of the Almighty.

EHIYEH: As alluded to in connection with the name SHADDAI, it is scarcely necessary to add that Moses himself possessed an inwardly deeper and more intimate knowledge of God than what he was called upon to manifest to the Egyptians. This becomes evident if we consider that when YHVH resolved to destroy the people of Israel for having turned away from Him in favor of the golden calf at the foot of Mt. Sinai, Moses asked instead that he himself might be blotted out from the Book of Life, and the people of Israel be spared. And in fact he did gain pardon for them. His willingness to be sacrificed manifests his deeper, more interior understanding of the divine. Here was no question of omnipotence, but of love and readiness for self-sacrifice. In the dialogue that resulted in the saving pardon of the people of Israel, under what name did God make Himself known to Moses? Was not the highest name of God revealed to Moses? Was not his soul set afire with the knowledge of this name, the *very name* that would on one occasion, long after the time of Moses, be *legitimately* spoken by Him who said: "Before Abraham was, I am"? We can also say that it was *because* Moses had declared his readiness to die for the people of Israel that he (together with Elijah) was found worthy to take part in the dialogue on Mt. Tabor with the Transfigured One—the *actual* bearer of this name—about His mission to sacrifice Himself for humanity.

On the other hand, *only* the One who had earlier chosen Abraham as father of the people in which He wished to appear could propose to Moses that he replace Abraham and become patriarch of a *new* people. And is not the "I am, before Abraham was" the *same* One who chose and appointed Abraham as patriarch of the people in which He wanted in due time to incarnate as Man?

The most mysterious name of God, the "I am" (EHI-YEH) revealed to Moses, is none other than the name of Christ *before* His appearance as the Son of Man. In his dialogue with God that led to the pardon of the people of Israel, Moses addressed himself *in fact* to Christ, "Who was in the beginning with God and was God." (John 1:1)

YAH (JAH): There is a name of God in both the Bible and in the tradition of the Kabbalah that unites the two names of the highest level—"I am" (EHIYEH) and "He is" (YHVH)—in that it has a part in both. This is the name YAH or JAH (יה), a name not often mentioned in the Scriptures, although it does appear in the "song" of Moses (Exodus 15:2):

> *Fortitudo et laus mea YAH, et factus est mihi in salutem.*
>
> The Lord (YAH) is my strength and my song, and He has become my salvation.

The name YAH represents the principle of redemption for the period extending from the *destruction of the Temple* until the *coming of the Messiah*. For example, the psalms contain the instruction:

> *Scribantur haec in generatione altera, et populus, qui cre-abitur, laudabit YAH.*

> Let this be recorded for a generation to come, so that a people yet unborn may praise the LORD (YAH). (Psalms 102:18)

And in the book of the prophet Malachi, the following prophecy is given: "Behold, I will send you Elijah." (Mal. 4:5) Here the name Eli-Jah (Eli-Yah)[1] itself contains this name of God (meaning "My God is YAH"), referring to the prophet who in the time of preparation for the coming of the "Anointed One" of God, the Messiah, is to be called upon and revered.

Generally, the name YAH is understood to be a contraction of the tetragrammaton YHVH. But consider for a moment: to contract the unutterable holy name for the sake of simplifying its pronunciation is manifestly unthinkable if we but call to mind that, whether pronounceable or not, it was in any case forbidden to utter it! Furthermore, as regards the thesis that there was a need to contract the holy name as an *aide-mémoire*, under what possible circumstances (even if one knew so holy a name) could such risk

---

[1] To avoid confusion, the "j" often seen in the English transliterations Jahveh/Jahweh is voiced "y." But in similar cases, such as Jehovah, Jacob, and Jesus, the "j" *is* voiced, whereas the proper Semitic pronunciation would be Yehovah, Yacob, and Yesus or Yeshua. Likewise, Elijah would be pronounced Eliyah—a voicing in fact preserved frequently in English in the form Elias, that is, Eli(y)as.

of forgetting it arise as to recommend the expediency of an abbreviated version? Surely, if the name of God was contracted, it could only have been to feature its most essential aspect for the purpose of meditating upon it with all the more focus!

Looked at this way, we may take the name YAH as the sound of the *sacred cipher* of the Incarnation of God, which according to its directing intention is actually "incarnated" in the name YAH. That is, the divine name YAH brings to expression both in its letter forms and in its pronunciation *God's directing will for redemption*. As concerns humanity, then, YAH may be considered the most important element in the full divine name YHVH—which accounts for its contraction to YH (Yod-Hé) = YAH. Here, likewise, we have the explanation for the traditional view that YAH expressed in particular the directing intention of the *time of preparation* for the coming of the Messiah, as we see expressly in the name for the one who "prepares the way," Elijah (Eli-Yah).

According to the *Zohar*, the name YAH is the most mysterious of all the holy names, for it designates the *source* of the divine stream where "the Yod gives its light to the Hé, which grants nourishment to the world below." The union of Yod with Hé is the source of the divine stream of blessing. We need only consider how Yod signifies the original, creative Oneness, and how Hé signifies the breath of life, in order to see as an image for the name YAH the radiating sun, the "sun of compassion" that shines upon all, just and unjust alike. Thus did it come to pass that Moses effected the pardon of the people of Israel by his appeal to the aspect of God revealed in the name YAH.

ELOHIM: The name ELOHIM is the name of God considered as the One who completed the work of Creation in six days. In the *first* chapter of Genesis this name appears thirty-two times, whereas the name YAHVEH ELOHIM appears for the first time only in the *second* chapter. (Genesis 2:4)

The singular of ELOHIM (אלוה) is ELOHA (אלהים), but it seldom appears in the Bible. We find it in Deuteronomy (32:15), in the book of Job, in the book of Isaiah, and in the book of Kings. ELOHA consists of the name EL joined with the final two letters of the name YAHVEH. The name ELOHA has the meaning "Master" in the sense of Master of the work of art that is Nature—or, we could also say, Creator of Nature.

Knowing this much, we are in a position to solve the riddle of the plurality expressed in the name ELOHIM, which as we can readily see would signify something like "many-sided mastery of the Master revealing itself in the work of the Creation." This understanding of the name ELOHIM goes far beyond the commonly advanced opinion that its plural form is nothing more than a case of the *pluralis majestatis*.[2] And it also does full justice to the decidedly monotheistic view of the Bible, which the literal translation of the ELOHIM as "gods" would clearly contradict, even were it linguistically admissible.

The point is that, in its plural form, ELOHIM does not denote a *multiplicity* of creators but an astonishing, unimaginably *many-sided* creative capacity on the part of the

---

[2] The majestic plural being the use of a plural personal pronoun to refer honorifically to a single person or entity.

One Creator, as revealed in the Creation. Thus the Kabbalah speaks of thirty-two paths of wisdom, an indication grounded in turn upon the fact that the name ELOHIM appears thirty-two times in the first chapter of the Genesis account of the Creation. There is no mention here of thirty-two *gods*, but of thirty-two *paths of wisdom* by which the all-encompassing Wisdom of the Creator is revealed in the Creation. In sum, we ought not to see in the name ELOHIM a multiplicity of authors of the Creation, but the many-sidedness of the Creative Wisdom of the *One* Author of the Creation.

As in the case of the other names of God, ELOHIM can also be used correctly or misused. Its *correct use* would be as a focus for meditation on the many-sidedness of the Wisdom of God as revealed in Creation—a meditation, therefore, occupied with the thirty-two paths of Wisdom. By contrast, its *misuse* would consist in analytically splintering the Godhead into a multiplicity of independent gods, as was generally done by the pagan peoples. In truth, it was not without some justification that the word ELOHIM was sometimes applied also to gods of the pagan religions, and indeed even to individuals who led their courts of justice. The Bible reports numerous cases of the misuse of the divine name ELOHIM in association with degeneration into polytheism, particularly with reference to the cults of the Baalim (plural of Baal) and the Phoenician goddess Astaroth or Astarte (equivalent to the Ishtar of the Assyro-Babylonian peoples).

Properly conceived, ELOHIM may be considered the unity (discernible within the multiplicity of differing revelations) of the many-sided mastery of the Master at work creatively in His Creation. Put another way, just as the image of the radiating sun corresponds to the divine name YAH, so does the image of the rainbow correspond to the divine name ELOHIM.

ELOHIM (YAHVEH) SABAOTH: Moving on, the idea of unity in multiplicity as the unanimous accord of the many under the sway of an overarching leadership is well expressed in the divine names ELOHIM SABAOTH and YAHVEH SABAOTH, both translated as "Lord, God of Hosts" (*Dominus Deus Sabaoth*). This name refers to God as Apex of the pyramid of the hierarchical world-order, as Chief of all hierarchical beings: angels, archangels, principalities, powers, virtues, dominions, thrones, cherubim, and seraphim.

To see God as the "Highest One" above the choirs of the spiritual hierarchies is to even more keenly revere His exaltedness. Indeed, to this day, such reverence for God's cosmic exaltation fills Christian cathedrals in the resounding of the words:

> *Sanctus, sanctus, sanctus Dominus Deus Sabaoth. Pleni sunt coeli et terra gloria tua. Hosanna in excelsis.*
>
> Holy, holy, holy, Lord, God of Hosts. Heaven and earth are filled with Your glory. Hosanna in the highest.

ADONAI: We turn now, finally, to the divine name ADONAI (אדוני), usually translated Lord (*Dominus, Kyrios*). This name refers to the experience of the God "of Hosts"—that is, of God beheld *through* the choir of the divine hierarchies, as their Superior. ADONAI is the name spoken *in place of* YHVH when the Scriptures are read. This is why the vowel signs for ADONAI are placed beneath the consonants of the name YHVH. This in turn gives rise to the name YEHOVAH (JEHOVAH). Sometimes, but less frequently, the vowel signs for the word ELOHIM, rather than ADONAI, are placed under the name YHVH. This gives rise, then, to the name YEHOVIH (JEHOVIH). But generally the divine name YHVH is replaced by ADONAI, which designates God as Master of the "world household."

ADONAI is essentially and by rights possessor and ruler of the world, the "LORD of the World." The world is His, and all beings of the world are His servants. However, they are *not* His servants on account of His *omnipotence* compelling their subservience (that is, the quality of the name SHADDAI) or because He is *superior* to the beings of the world (that is, the quality of the name EL), but because as the eternal LORD His *glory* induces all beings to commit themselves to Him, to serve Him, to be obedient to Him.

What the Lord of Hosts (ELOHIM SABAOTH) is in the *heavenly* world, the LORD (ADONAI) is in the *natural* world, the world of facts and events.

The Sephiroth

A deeper understanding of the names of God according to their inner context is scarcely possible without knowledge of the traditional teaching of the ten *sephiroth*, which occupies a key position in the Kabbalah. The word *sephirah* (plural: *sephiroth*) means "number." Here it is not a matter, however, of number in a quantitative sense, but in the sense of the opening words of the book *Sepher Yetzirah*:

> YAH, the Lord of Hosts, the Living God, King of the Universe, Omnipotent, All-Kind and Merciful,

Supreme and Extolled, who is Eternal, Sublime and
Most Holy, ordained (formed) and created the Uni-
verse in thirty-two mysterious paths of wisdom by
three Sepharim, namely: (1) S'for; (2) Sippur; and (3)
Sapher, which are in Him, one and the same.[3]

Here the concept "number" signifies "mode of creation."
Analogically speaking, just as it can be said that there are
various categories of *knowledge* (Aristotle put forward ten
such), so in a certain sense do the sephiroth signify ten categories of *creation*. The sephiroth are the stages of transition
(or, the connecting links) between the Creator and the created world, between the Absolute and Relative. In their
totality, the sephiroth map out the paths of transition from
the archetypal world of God to the moral world of the soul,
and from the latter to the outer world of physical facts.
Thus the system of the sephiroth (the so-called sephiroth
tree) is divided into four spheres or worlds: the world of
emanation (*olam ha atziluth*), the world of creation (*olam
ha briah*), the world of structure or formation (*olam ha
yetzirah*), and the world of activity (*olam ha assiah*). Furthermore, these four worlds correspond to the four letters
of the tetragrammaton: Yod (world of emanation), Hé
(world of creation), Vau (world of formation), and second
Hé (world of activity).

---

[3] *Sepher Yezirah* I, 1; published in the original Hebrew and translated
by Isidor Kalisch (New York: L.H. Frank, 1877), 14. Kalisch adds in a
footnote (50): "These Sepharim or three words of similar expression signify: (1) number, calculation, or idea; (2) the word; (3) the writing of the
word. The idea, word, and writing (of the word) are signs to man for a
thing, and are not the thing itself; to the Creator, however, idea, word,
and writing (of the word) are the thing itself."

The ten sephiroth, which themselves belong to the world of emanation, nevertheless extend into all four worlds. The three highest sephiroth, *kether* (crown), *chokmah* (wisdom), and *binah* (understanding) belong exclusively to the world of emanation. The next three, *chesed* (mercy, majesty, expansion, also called *gedulah*), *geburah* (power, judgment, also called *din*), and *tiphareth* (beauty) extend to the world of creation. The following three, *netzach* (triumph), *hod* (glory), and *yesod* (foundation) extend to the world of formation. And the last, the tenth, sephirah, *malkuth* (kingdom), which marks the realization of the nine higher ones within the world of action, is the only one of the sephiroth extending to that world.

The ten sephiroth are grouped together in the form of a tree, which for this reason is called the kabbalistic or sephiroth tree. The four sephiroth *kether* (crown), *tiphareth* (beauty), *yesod* (foundation), and *malkuth* (kingdom) form the trunk of the tree (also called the middle pillar). The other six sephiroth, laid out to the right and left sides of the trunk, are called branches. They form, alongside the middle pillar, the right and the left pillars. The right pillar is that of mercy or compassion, the left pillar that of strict justice or righteousness. Thus, the three sephiroth wisdom, mercy, and triumph form the right pillar, and the three sephiroth understanding, power, and glory the left pillar. The middle pillar, which represents the synthesis of the right and left pillars, is formed (as we have said) of the sephiroth crown, beauty, foundation, and kingdom.

The sephiroth tree is also called "primordial man" (*adam kadmon*). Crown, wisdom, and understanding, the three uppermost sephiroth, form his head; mercy and power, the two arms; beauty, the trunk or torso; triumph and glory, the

The Sephiroth Tree

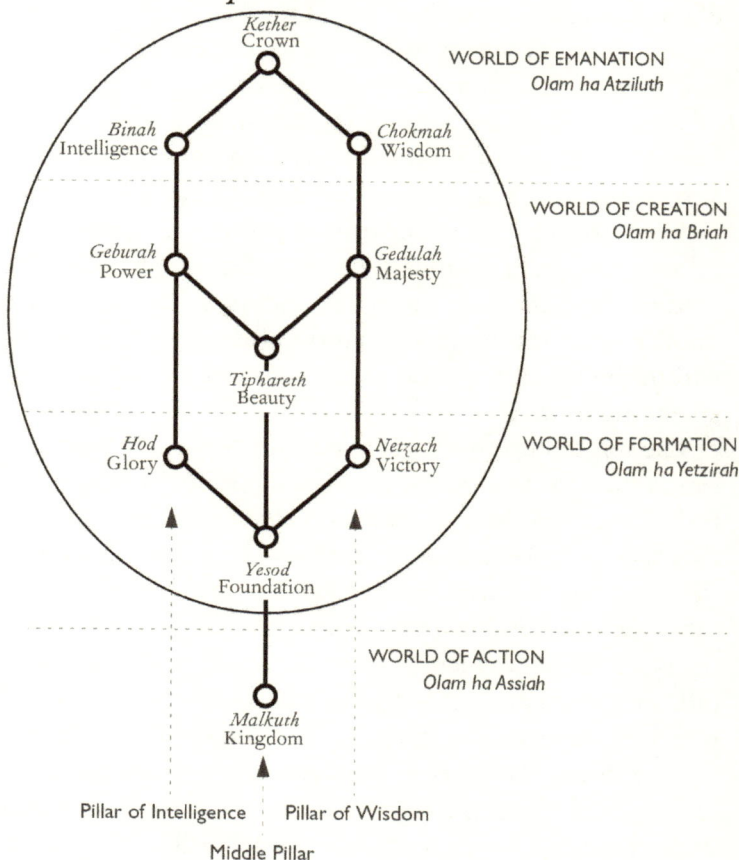

two hips; foundation, the organs of procreation; and king-dom, the feet.

The first sephirah, the crown, is the primal and highest of all divine manifestations. According to the *Zohar*:

> It is the principle of all principles, the secret wisdom, the most exalted crown, with which all diadems and

all crowns are embellished. (*Zohar*, III, 288b) The divine name corresponding to the crown is EHIYEH ("I am"), because it is Being. For this reason the first sephirah has been called the primal point, or simply the point: "When the most Hidden of the Hidden wished to reveal Himself, He formed first a single point. . . . For so long as this point of light had not left His Bosom, the Unlimited (*Ain Soph*) remained entirely unknown and shed no light." (*Zohar*, I, 2a) Then forth from His Bosom proceeded concurrently two seemingly opposed but in truth inseparable principles: one *masculine* and active, called wisdom (*chokmah*); the other *feminine* and passive, called understanding (*binah*). Wisdom is also called the *father*, for, as is said: wisdom *begets* all things. Understanding, then, is the *mother*, as is written: "You are to name understanding *mother*." (*Zohar*, III, 290a) From this mysterious and eternal union is born a *son*, who, as manifestation of the primal point, takes on the characteristics of the father and the mother, in this way bearing testimony to both. This son of wisdom and understanding, with his twofold inheritance from the primal point, is called also the first-born one, and also *cognition* or *knowledge* (*daath*).[4]

Let us cite also this remarkable passage from the *Commentary to the Zohar* by Moses of Cordova:

The first three sephiroth—crown, wisdom, and understanding—must be seen as one and the same thing. The first represents *cognition* or *knowledge*, the

[4] Adolphe Franck, *Die Kabbala oder die Religions-Philosophie der Hebräer* (from the French, revised by A. Gelinek, Leipzig, 1844, 137).

second the *knower*, the third *that which is known*. To explain this identity one must know that the knowing of the Creator is not like that of created beings; for with them, knowing is different from the subject of knowledge, even as, likewise, their knowing relates to objects that, again, differ from the subject. This is indicated by the expressions: thinking, thinker, and that which is thought. In contrast, the Creator is simultaneously knowing, knower, and that which is known. In fact, *His* manner of knowing does not consist in Him directing His thinking to things outside of Him; in that He Himself thinks and is knowing, He knows everything and sees everything that is. Nothing exists that is not one with Him, and that does not subsist in His own substance. He is the prototype of every being, and all beings are in Him in their purest and complete form, so that the perfection of created beings actually exists in the mind of that Perfect One who, in the process of begetting them, united Himself with them; and to the extent they distance themselves from Him, they also fall away from that perfect and exalted state. Thus the form of all varieties of being in this world is in the sephiroth, and the form of the sephiroth is in the source from which they flow.[5]

The entire system of the sephiroth can also be represented as three triangles that reach full realization when brought together and united in the kingdom (*malkuth*), as follows:

The first triangle (pointing upward), formed from the active–passive polarity of wisdom (*chokmah*) and understanding (*binah*) reaches its point of synthesis in the crown

---

[5] *Pardes Rimonim* ("Orchard of Pomegranates"), 55a.

(*kether*): it belongs to the world of emanation (*olam ha atziluth*). The second triangle (pointing downward), formed from the polarity of mercy (*chesed* or *gedulah*) and power (*geburah* or *din*), reaches its point of synthesis in beauty (*tiphareth*): it belongs to the world of creation (*olam ha briah*). The third triangle (also pointing downward), formed from the polarity of triumph (*netzach*) and glory (*hod*), reaches its point of synthesis in foundation (*yesod*): it belongs to the world of formation (*olam ha yetzirah*). The last and tenth sephirah, kingdom (*malkuth*), brings to fulfillment the harmony of the nine higher sephiroth in the world of activity (*olam ha assiah*).

The names of the ten sephiroth as translated into Latin by Athanasius Kircher, S.J. in his work *Oedipus Aegyptiacus* are given below, along with the ten divine names ascribed to them:

Kether	Summa Corona
Chokmah	Summa Sapienta
Binah	Intelligentia sive Spiritus Sanctus
Chesed (*Gedulah*)	Misericordia
Geburah (*Din*)	Timor
Tiphareth	Pulchritudo
Netzach	Victoria
Hod	Honor seu Gloria
Yesod	Fundamentum
Malkuth	Regnum

Kether	EHIYEH ("I am")
Chokmah	YAH or YHVH
Binah	ELOHIM or YHVH-ELOHIM

Chesed (*Gedulah*)	EL
Geburah (*Pachad/Din*)	ELOHIM-GIBOR ("Mighty One")
Tiphareth	ELOHA or YHVH
Netzach	YHVH-SABAOTH
Hod	ELOHIM-SABAOTH
Yesod	SHADDAI or EL-HAIA
Malkuth	ADONAI

Most probably these are also the ten mystical names of God of which St. Jerome speaks in his letter to Marcella.[6] They may serve as a stimulus for meditative work, i.e., "thinking with the head and the heart."

[6] St. Jerome in his letter (XXV) to Marcella regarding the ten divine names [given with no further commentary]: "An explanation of the ten names given to God in the Hebrew Scriptures. The ten names are El, Elohim, Sabaoth, Elion, Asher yeheyeh (Exodus 3:14), Adonai, Yah, the tetragram YHVH, and Shaddai. Written at Rome AD 384."

THE
FOURTH
COMMANDMENT

"Remember the Sabbath Day, to Keep It Holy"

The Law of Recollection and Return

"Remember the sabbath day by keeping it holy. Six days you shall labor and do all your work, but the seventh day is a sabbath to the LORD your God. . . . For in six days the LORD made the heavens and the earth, the sea, and all that is in them, but he rested on the seventh day. Therefore the LORD blessed the sabbath day and made it holy."   Exodus 20:8–11

HE SYSTEM OF THE NAMES OF GOD AND THE sephiroth that we considered in the preceding chapter offers us an opportunity and stimulus to think through them further meditatively, that is (as we have said), with a thinking in which head and heart resonate together. The system of the ten names of God and the ten sephiroth may serve as a framework for such meditative work, as a kind of "syllabus" for a schooling in meditation on the rulership of God and on the stages and pathways of that rulership as revealed in the Bible and in the spiritual history of humankind. In fact, this framework or syllabus has already long served as a meditative schooling in the kabbalistic tradition. Such schooling has nothing to do with adhering to the teachings of Old Testament mystical theology, or of becoming a "believer" in the Kabbalah. On the contrary, it is simply a matter of taking seriously the results of profound meditation on the Old Testament (results acquired over many centuries by generations of students of the Kabbalah) and thinking them through ourselves with a view to their fruitfulness.

Since the Old Testament is a part of the Bible, the Kabbalah ought to be taken just as seriously as a means for understanding it as is Christian mystical theology for understanding the New Testament. Understanding the Bible as a *whole* requires of those committed to its meditative study that they embrace as well the results of the research and meditative insights of all who have devoted themselves to such study: Church teachers and theologians, Kabbalists, and Hasidists. Those serious about fathoming the whole of Holy Scripture to a depth fully worthy of it will scarcely allow themselves to ignore the *Sepher Yetzirah* or the *Zohar*, just as little as they would the *Miscellanies* of Clement of Alexandria or the *Homilies* and *Commentaries* of Origen on the gospels.

Meditation: "Hallowing the Sabbath"

The word *meditatio*, which is also sometimes used in the sense of *consideratio* (for example by St. Bernard of Clairvaux), indicates a state of heightened wakefulness of the capacity for insight (thinking), for empathy (feeling), and for evaluation (willing). In other words, meditation is the inner, contemplative life of a soul unreservedly devoted to the search for *truth*. At the same time, meditation is a turning-away from the outer world: its concerns, its influences, its after-effects, as well as memories thereof. A master of meditation, contemplation, and prayer, St. Bernard of Clairvaux, says:

> Meditation (reflection) first purifies its own source, i.e., the soul, from which it arises. Then it regulates the inclinations, directs activity, moderates excess, shapes morals, makes life honest and regulated, and mediates knowledge of divine as well as human things. It is this that replaces confusion with order, checks the inclination to lose oneself in uncertainty, gathers together that which is dispersed, penetrates into that which is hidden, discovers that which is true, distinguishes it from that which merely appears as such, and brings to light fiction and lie.
>
> Further, it is meditation that determines beforehand what is to be done and brings that which has been done to consciousness, so that nothing remains in the soul that is in need of clarification and correction. Likewise, it is meditation that enables misfortune to be foreseen even when happiness prevails; and that makes it possible during misfortune to preserve an attitude of not being dejected. It is the source of courage on the one hand and of prudence (*prudentia*) on the other.[1]

---

[1] Bernard of Clairvaux, *De Consideratione* I, 7. He wrote this treatise between 1149 and 1152 for Pope Eugene III.

Regarding the difference between meditation (reflection) and contemplation (beholding), St. Bernard says:

> Pay attention to what I mean by meditation (reflection). One should not conceive of meditation as being synonymous with contemplation in every respect. In fact, contemplation presupposes the truth it recognizes as being certain, whereas use is made of meditation (reflection) for finding this truth. Understood in this sense, it seems to me that contemplation can be defined as true and certain intuition of the spirit of any reality whatsoever, or also as grasping that which is true and that eliminates doubt. As far as meditation is concerned, it is the intensive effort of thinking, the striving of the soul searching for what is true. Nevertheless, it is customary to use both designations indiscriminately, whether one is dealing with meditation or contemplation.[2]

The Holy Abbot of Clairvaux, then, sees the fruits of meditation in the four virtues,[3] which are the basis, not just for the life of monks of contemplative orders, but also for all life worthy of being called human. In other words, anyone who strives "to know what he does" ought to dedicate a certain time for inner remembrance, for observing and judging from a higher vantage point his life and striving. For, in order not merely to be swept along by life's flow, but

[2] Ibid. II, 2.

[3] That is, the four *cardinal* virtues: prudence, justice, fortitude, and temperance. Unlike the three *theological* virtues (faith, hope, and love), which are gifts of God through grace, the four cardinal virtues can be practiced by anyone, and thus represent the basis of natural morality.

also to be in a position to direct our life creatively, we must be able to step back periodically from the stream of daily life. To express this truth in biblical language, we need only recall the words of the fourth commandment:

> Remember the sabbath day by keeping it holy. Six days you shall labor and do all your work, but the seventh day is a sabbath to the Lord your God. (Exodus 20:9–10)

While we dedicate the greater part of our time to the stream of daily life with its various tasks, duties, and other concerns, a seventh part of our time ought to be consecrated to turning within, to retreating reflectively from this stream. Meditation is "hallowing the sabbath." It is the fulfillment of the command to remember and to keep the sabbath holy. Meditation, contemplation, and prayer all belong to inner recollection or "hallowing the sabbath." They are three stages of interiorization: of thinking (meditation), of feeling (contemplation), of will (prayer). Interiorization is the goal and meaning of turning within, of recollective withdrawal. Again, this is what is meant by "hallowing the sabbath."

⊕

Now, the book of Genesis is quite explicit in showing that the rhythmic alternation between creative activity and contemplation *mirrors* the rhythmic alternation of the divine work of creation and rest. The resting that follows upon God's creative work is, then, the "interiorizing" of that preceding work. Thus, Genesis reports that, upon His completion of the creative work on each of the six days, "God saw that it was good (*tov*)." That is, by interrupting His creative work after each day, the Creator established the *divine archetype* of meditation, setting the divine example of the contemplative turning-within that is meditation. At the core of the interior, divine-moral assessment ("God saw that it was good") of each completed day's creative work lay an interiorized "recapitulation" of the work completed on that day:

> And God saw everything that He had made, and behold, it was very good. And there was evening and there was morning, a sixth day (Genesis 1:31). . . . And on the seventh day God finished His work which He had done, and He rested on the seventh day from all His work which he had done. (Genesis 2:2)

And the "great rest" of the seventh day, which consisted of the interiorized recapitulation of the entire preceding six days' work, took the form of *blessing*:

> God blessed the seventh day and hallowed it. (Genesis 2:3)

Thus we see in the Genesis report of Creation the divine sounding-together of three motifs: God creates through His Word; God turns within to interiorly affirm the goodness of His created work; God blesses that work during this period of interiorization.

Furthermore, just as the Word is inseparable from the Creator's work of *creation*, so is the Spirit inseparable from the results of the Creator's periods of *interiorization*. At the outset we have the Creator (Father), whose will is brought to realization by the creative Word (Son); then the interior withdrawal whereby the creative activity of the Father and of the Son is affirmed ("found to be good"); and finally the Spirit (Holy Spirit), who in the course of the interior withdrawal illuminates the meaning and value of what has been created.

To summarize: The world was created from the Father through the Son, and was blessed by the Holy Spirit. Clearly, then, the blessing of the Holy Spirit that followed upon the periods of interior withdrawal between the days of Creation is just as much a part of the story of Creation as the account of its primal origin is the realization by the Word of the Father's will. In other words, the periods of *interior withdrawal* belong as much to the fundamental truth and divine law of the Creation as does its original coming into being from the creative will of the Father through the creative Word of the Son.

⊕

Now, the alternating rhythm of creative activity and interior withdrawal (a rhythm established, as we have just seen, by the Godhead) forms the basis not only of the Mosaic story of the Creation, but of the wisdom of India, which also speaks of a universal cosmic law whereby the Godhead of the world alternates between such periods. For its part, the Hindu teaching tells of "days" and "nights" of Brahma (the Creator). These alternating periods of Brahma's *creative* outbreathing and *interiorizing* inbreathing are called *manvantaras* and *pralayas*. This divine-cosmic rhythm is equally the model, archetype, and cause of the rhythm of *our* breathing, which is in turn the primary basis for the practice of focused breathing in yoga, which is nothing else than a conscious experiencing of the alternating conditions of turning outward and turning within, of activity and retreat, of outer engagement and meditation. In biblical language, the former consists of participation in the creative work of the world, and the latter consists of the periodic recurrence of interiorization, which is to say of the "celebration of the world sabbath."

St. Bernard of Clairvaux, speaking out of his vast experience, presents the practice of interior withdrawal as indispensable for establishing and maintaining a way of life that is truly worthy of humanity—that is, his approach is "anthropological." By contrast, the approach taken by the traditional wisdom of India is "cosmic-metaphysical." Then again there is the recent English researcher and philosopher of history Arnold J. Toynbee, who discovered and put forward in considerable detail yet another approach, that of the universally valid "psychological and cultural-historical" law of repeated interior withdrawals and subsequent returns in the spiritual life of humankind. For his part, Toynbee proceeded from a comparative study of the individual biographies of representatives of the "creative" minority who exert epoch-making influences on the cultural life of society. He then looked for, and found, analogous effects of the law of withdrawal and return in the development of human society itself:

> In terms of the personality's external relations with the society to which he belongs, we shall be describing the same duality of movement [that we have called] withdrawal and return. The withdrawal makes it possible for the personality to realize powers within himself that might have remained dormant if he had not been released for the time being from his social toils and trammels. Such a withdrawal may be a voluntary action on his part, or it may be forced upon him by circumstances beyond his control; in either

case, the withdrawal is an opportunity, and perhaps a necessary condition, for the anchorite's transfiguration; "anchorite," in the original Greek, means literally "one who goes apart"; but a transfiguration in solitude can have no purpose, and perhaps even no meaning, except as a prelude to the return of the transfigured personality into the social milieu out of which he had originally come: a native environment from which the human social animal cannot permanently estrange himself without repudiating his humanity and becoming, in Aristotle's phrase, "either a beast or a god." The return is the essence of the whole movement as well as its final cause.[4]

Toynbee sees in Moses's lonely ascent up Mt. Sinai a significant link between withdrawal and returning:

> Moses ascends the mountain in order to commune with Yahveh at Yahveh's call; and the call is to Moses alone, while the rest of the Children of Israel are charged to keep their distance. Yet Yahveh's whole purpose in calling Moses up is to send him down again as the bearer of a new law which Moses is to communicate to the rest of the people because they are incapable of coming up and receiving the communication themselves.[5]

On another front, Toynbee tells us of the fourteenth-century Arab thinker Ibn Khaldun, who left an account of the Prophet Muhammad's experience and mandate, which also

---

[4] A.J. Toynbee, *A Study of History* (Oxford: Oxford University Press, new edition, 1987), 217.
[5] Ibid.

strongly emphasizes return to the world after withdrawal from it has taken place:

> The human soul has an innate disposition to divest itself of its human nature in order to clothe itself in the nature of the angels and to become an angel in reality for a single instant of time—a moment which comes and goes as swiftly as the flicker of an eyelid. Thereupon the soul resumes its human nature, after having received, in a world of angels, a message which it has to carry to its own human kind.[6]

Further, Toynbee indicates the significance of withdrawal and return in the life of Jesus, which also finds its expression in the expectation of the return of the Resurrected One from his Ascension into heaven: after the great withdrawal marked by his Ascension, his return or Reappearance is to take place. Toynbee points also to the life of the apostle Paul, who, after his sudden conversion on the way to Damascus, went into the Arabian desert for three years. Only after this withdrawal did he meet with the elder apostles in order to take up his work in community with them. The life of St. Benedict is similar: he lived a solitary life for three years before returning to society to take charge of a group of monks, first in the valley of Subiaco, then on Monte Cassino. St. Gregory the Great also underwent a retreat of three years, after which he began to convert the pagan English. He was later called back to Rome, held various church offices, and was elected pope (590–604).

Turning now to the East, Siddhartha Gautama, the historical Buddha, lived for seven years in retreat, which bore

---

[6] Ibid., 218.

fruit at his enlightenment under the Bodhi tree with his resolve to share his insight with his fellowmen. This made him the central focus and head of a brotherhood, and founder of one of the great world religions.

In the case of Muhammad (570–632), withdrawal and return formed the prelude to two decisive turning-points in his life. The first, which led to strict monotheism, took place after an approximately fifteen-year period of retreat, during which he led the life of a caravan merchant trafficking between Arabian oases. The second, that of proclaiming an all-encompassing religious-political law, began with his withdrawal: the *Hegira* (*Hijra*), or emigration. He withdrew from his home oasis Mecca to the oasis Yathrib, which ever since has been called Medina (*Medinat-el-Rabi*, meaning "city of the prophet"). This latter period of withdrawal is regarded by Muslims as so decisive a turning-point that they reckon time from it: their year one begins with Muhammad's flight from Mecca, whither he returned seven years later, this time as lord and master of half of Arabia.

⊕

The essential teaching of all these historical figures is that humankind's creative life and activity is founded upon a succession of periods of contraction and expansion, of sabbath-days and work-days, of meditation and action. There is no breathing out without having first breathed in. Similarly, we cannot be creatively active if we have not first received, or awakened, the necessary power, insight, and enthusiasm by turning within to meditation, contemplation, and prayer. In the final analysis, the essence and the secret of creativity lies in the power and the capacities we owe to the blessing of the seventh day—the World-Sabbath.

THE
FIFTH
COMMANDMENT

"Honor Your
Father and Your Mother"

The Law of Continuity,
or The Life of Tradition

"Honor your father and your mother, so that
you may live long in the land the LORD your
God is giving you."
                              Exodus 20:12

I

The Divine Foundation and
Archetype of Fatherhood and Motherhood

HE MOST PRECIOUS AND NEEDFUL EXPERIENCE
anyone can have on this earth, from earliest
childhood, is love; more specifically, parental
love, lacking which we could not make a start in
life or remain alive. As is well known, a newborn child can
thrive only if loving, caring, protecting hands receive and
cherish it. Nourishment, warmth, and protection—already
given in the mother's body before birth—remain a life
necessity to the child in manifold ways after birth also.
Moreover, the child needs both to be heard and to hear the
voices of others. The child needs language for its develop-

ment because it requires contact, communication, and interaction, which are, in turn, fundamental to the first stirrings of thinking, understanding, and being understood.

With the further unfolding of the child's body and soul, the distinction between mother-love and father-love begins to emerge more clearly. Mother-love tends toward an enveloping quality that "carries" the child further until the "full-term" of maturity is reached. Father-love tends toward stimulating and accelerating the child's development and independence. Father-love sees in the child an "heir" to continue his life's work, to fight for the same ideal and to further the same task. Mother-love stays true to the image of the original mother–child bond of the pre-natal period: enveloping, protecting, and sustaining. Mother-love seeks to protect the child from life's roughness, to preserve it from disappointment and sorrow, to turn its every tear into a smile. The loving mother holds the child in her embrace, pressed to her heart, for decades on end—perhaps until death and beyond. Embracing the child is certainly not foreign to father-love, but shows itself less often: in solemn moments of heartfelt sharing, grateful mutual acknowledgement, taking pride in one another.

Parental love, the love bestowed by both father and mother, represents the most precious, meaningful experience a child can have on earth. It is the dowry the child will carry through life, the "capital" of soul-warmth and soul-light upon which the developing individual can draw for a lifetime. Parental love prepares us, by natural analogy, to comprehend divine love, or at least to gain some presentiment of it, so that we may hope to understand the depth and truth of St. John's words: "God is love, and he who abides in love abides in God, and God abides in him."

(1 John 4:16) For as God is love, so must the foundation
and archetype of all love, including parental love, be in God.

⊕

Now, if fatherhood and father-love have their origin and
foundation in the Godhead, and correspond in essence to
the love of God the Father (as all Christians believe, even
Protestants who have separated themselves from the stream
of living tradition of the Church), how can we justify leaving unanswered the question whether, correspondingly,
motherhood and mother-love have their origin and foundation in the Godhead also? Are we to deny that mother-love
is rooted in the divine, that it has its archetype in the divine,
and esteem only father-love as worthy of a divine archetype?
We find a categorical answer to this question in the prayer-
life and devotions of the tradition of the Church. Indeed,
acknowledgment of the maternal principle plays a fundamental role in the religious practices of both Catholic and
Orthodox Christianity.

Praying the rosary has for centuries been intrinsic to the
religious life of the Catholic Church. And essential to the
rosary is the fact that its sequence of prayers appeals alter-
nately to father-love (in the form of the Our Father, with
which each set of rosary prayers dedicated to the various
mysteries begins) and to mother-love (in the form of the
ten Hail Marys that follow). In the Orthodox Church, veneration of the Mother of God goes so far that in the liturgy
the hymn is sung:

> Truly it is worthy to bless Thee, the Theotokos,
> ever blessed and pure, and the Mother of our God.
> Thee, who art more honorable than the cherubim,

and incomparably more glorious than the seraphim;
who incorruptibly didst bear God, the Word,
verily the Theotokos we magnify.

For the Orthodox, then, the Mother of God ranks above
the highest of the angelic hierarchies—the cherubim and
seraphim—and so belongs to the supra-hierarchical realm
of the Godhead. Now, above the cherubim and seraphim,
highest of the hierarchies, stands the eternal Trinity of God.

Before saying more on this theme, however, it must be
emphasized that what we are speaking of now is not a matter
of Church *dogma*. Rather, we are pointing out the measure
of *devotion* displayed by Orthodox believers toward Mary as
Holy Mother: for the hearts of the faithful in Russia (the
land where the author of these pages was born and raised),
Mary is Queen of Hearts because she is the symbol and
archetype of maternal love. The Orthodox Church also calls
Mary Queen of Heaven and Queen of the Angels.

Turning now to the Latin liturgy, we find that in the
readings for Mary's birth these words of the eternal Wisdom are given her to speak:

> The LORD created me at the beginning of his
> work. . . . When he established the heavens, I was
> there, when he drew a circle on the face of the
> deep . . . rejoicing in his inhabited world and delight-
> ing in the human race. (Proverbs 8:22, 27, 31)

Medieval depictions have Mary taking her seat next to the
exalted Christ and receiving the crown. The piety of the
people associates the veneration of the Heart of Mary with
the veneration of the Heart of Jesus. Instead of taking
offence at this, should we not follow the honored rubric *lex
orandi, lex credendi*, and ask, rather, what *truth* may stand

behind this insight that the maternal nature looking upon us in the person of Mary is primordially rooted in the depth of the Godhead?

⊕

The Jewish kabbalistic tradition also answers with a resounding yes the question whether, by nature and primordial foundation, mother-love is divine. The Kabbalah teaches, in accordance with the verse "God created man in His image and likeness . . . male and female He created them," that God has two aspects: masculine and feminine. It characterizes these as "countenances": the greater and the lesser. The greater countenance, or "ancient of days," is present in the sephirah *kether* (the crown) as the reflection of the "androgynous" Godhead, which is called *ain soph* (the unlimited). From *kether*, a process of polarization then gives rise to masculine and feminine principles. The right branch of the polarization is the masculine principle, the left branch is the feminine principle.

Thus, through the androgynous Godhead's reflected presence in *kether*—in the world of emanation (*olam ha atziluth*)—and its subsequent polarization in that world into the sephirot *chokmah* (wisdom) and *binah* (understanding), *ain soph* (the unlimited) comes to manifestation as *both* Father and Mother of Creation.

If we now follow this polarization further into the world of creation (*olam ha briah*), which is centered on the sephirah *tiphareth* or beauty, we find the masculine principle characterized as king or holy king (*melekh*) and the feminine principle (*shekinah* or glory: the divine presence in created being) characterized as matrona or queen. Just as the king (*melekh*) is likened to the sun, so is matrona or queen likened to the moon, as the reflection of ideal beauty. Matrona is also called Eve, for as the text tells us, Eve is mother of all things, and everything that exists on earth suckles at her breast and is blessed by her.[1]

The king and queen we are speaking of (also called the "two countenances") are a pair whose task it is to bestow upon the world ever-renewed graces, and, through their union, to continue the work of the Creation—in other words, to sustain that work everlastingly.

According to the *Zohar*, the soul viewed in its purest essence is rooted in understanding (*binah*), which is the highest "mother" principle. If the soul is to be *masculine* in quality, it moves on from *binah*, passing through the principle of grace or expansion (*chesed* or *gedulah*); if it is to be *feminine* in quality, it moves on from *binah*, passing through and taking into itself the principle of justice or contraction (*geburah*).

Finally, through the union of the king and queen (which as the text relates is, for the generation of the soul, what male and female are for the procreation of the body), the soul enters the world in which we as humankind live (*malkuth*).[2]

In light of this kabbalistic teaching (found also in Hasidism, on which Martin Buber is an authority) we will summarize below as best we may the metaphysical-religious foundation for the commandment: "Honor your father and your mother."

---

[1] *Zohar, Idra Zuta, ad finem* [that is, toward the end of the "Small Assembly," a text included in the Zohar].

[2] *Zohar,* III, 7.

Creation (that is, the world) owes its existence to the love of the eternal Father and the love of the eternal Mother. From their union proceeds "as Light from Light, God from God" the Son and the Daughter, designated as the holy king and the holy queen, who together direct the work of Creation, guiding it to ever deeper levels of interiorization.

The dimension of interiorization itself, however, does not fall under the direction of the Son and the Daughter in connection with their joint work—first of bringing Creation into being, and thereafter sustaining and guiding it toward that interior dimension. That is, the dimension of interiorization does not stand under the direction of the overall process of *becoming*. It is aligned instead with the *blessing* that proceeds from the "hallowing" or interiorizing Holy Spirit, Who does not proceed from the Son and Daughter (in the above sense) but rather from the Father and Son.

Corresponding, however, to the blessing of the *transcendent* interiorizing Holy Spirit of the Holy Trinity, is the blessing of the *immanent* interiorizing Presence—which we may call the Holy Soul, the Virgin of Israel, or the Soul of the community of Israel. She is the deeply moving and touching figure (as portrayed especially by Martin Buber) of the Weeping Virgin who accompanies the chosen people into exile (and not only in a geographical sense). It is She who stands behind the wailing wall in Jerusalem, behind the lamentation of all humanity.

In this way, kabbalistic tradition *extends* the teaching of the Holy Trinity itself! For it acknowledges that father-love and mother-love are of the same divine origin and value, as presupposed by the commandment: "Honor your father and your mother." In light of this extended teaching, the

Three-in-One of the Trinity becomes the Six-in-One or Double Trinity. But even so, the fundamental conception of *mono*theism is not lost thereby; rather, it remains just as valid in light of this Double Trinity as it has always remained in the Christian doctrine of the Trinity, or the Three-in-One Unity of God.

To the triangle of Father, Son, and Holy Spirit, then, we here add the triangle of Mother, Daughter, and Holy Soul: two triangles belonging inseparably together. Joined thus, they represent the six-pointed Star of David, or (according to kabbalistic tradition) the Seal of Solomon:

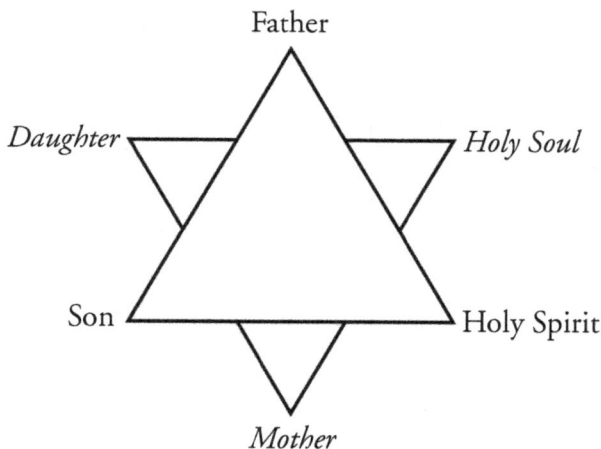

Father

Daughter   *Holy Soul*

Son   Holy Spirit

Mother

Regrettably, the National Socialists chose this symbol to brand the Jews a lesser race. Our great hope is that the above considerations will open a pathway of thinking and sympathetic understanding along which this symbol may come to be honored again in all its true depth and holiness. For it is a symbol of faithfulness to the commandment: "Honor your father and your mother—as in heaven, so also upon the earth."

II

The Law of Living Tradition

*(That your days may be long in the land
which the Lord your God gives you)*

Our native human reason would be unable to make anything of the world as empirically given if it did not have at its disposal the three fundamental categories or ways of ordering our experience that we call space, time, and causality. The simplest and most concrete description of these three categories would be: for *space*, that things are next to each other; for *time*, that things succeed each other; and for *causality*, that things exist because of each other.[3] Without these three categories, our reason would lack orientation. Indeed, it could not even frame questions, for all inquiry presupposes some combination of *where* (whither, whence), *when* (before, after), and *why* (wherefore, to what purpose). Furthermore, these three categories hold true not only for the empirical outer world but also for the realm of metaphysics, morality, values, and faith.

Moral Causality. For example, the disciples' question to Jesus regarding the man born blind (whether his blindness was owing to his own or to his parents' sin) presupposed the law of moral causality. In fact, it did so on two possible counts: either in the sense of the Mosaic pronouncement concerning the "sins of the fathers afflicting the children," or in the sense of the guilt of the man born blind himself. As we have pointed out before, the latter possibility corresponds to

---

[3] These three categories are expressed in the German in the lapidary expressions: *das Nebeneinander, das Nacheinander, das Wegeneinander.*

the conception generally held by peoples of the East called *karma*, according to which individuals themselves—and not their children or children's children—bear the consequences of their deeds, whether noble or ignoble. The deeper sense of the disciples' question, then, was whether the fate of the man born blind was causally connected with his parents' guilt, or with his own karma (his own prior guilt, whether in this life or in an existence before this life).

The answer Jesus gave the disciples was most remarkable, for it established the reality of another and very different form of causality—that is, that the destiny of the man born blind was neither the consequence of his *ancestors'* guilt (in the sense of retribution through heredity or moral causality working through the generations), nor atonement for his *own* guilt (through individual karma), but occurred, rather, in order that

God's works might be made manifest in him.
(John 9:3)

This means that the cause of his blindness lay, not in the past (whether generational or individual), but in the future! It was not a matter of past heredity or karma, but of *providence*. But even so, the disciples' question and the Master's reply both pertain to the fundamental category or ordering principle of causality, for the decrees of providence are by nature *causal* also, and thus have their *effects* as well—but with the *distinguo* that in the case of providence the causes and effects come from the future, not from the past. The deep truth of the Master's answer is that the cause of the man born blind's malady did not originate from human subjects (whether his parents' guilt or his own) but from a suprahuman Subject—that is, from God's providence.

Moral Space and Time. But it is not only the category of causality that can be understood in a purely moral sense. The same holds true of the categories of space and time. When, for example, we pray the opening salutation of the Lord's Prayer: "Our Father, who art in heaven," we do not mean by "heaven" the external space of planets and stars, but *moral* space—that is, a space in which nobility corresponds to height and baseness to depth. Similarly, the second part of the commandment: "Honor your father and your mother, that your days may be long in the land which the Lord your God gives you," is not meant to hold out the prospect of "living for a long time" at some spatially-determined place, but the *continuance* of what is for you most important in life—your ideas, ideals, and goals—within the sphere of influence granted them by God. In other words, in the text referred to it is not a question of promising a protracted earthly lifespan in some spatial setting, but rather that with respect to what is set in motion during our earthly life by way of actions and values (whether as individuals or collectivities), we may be assured of their continuing, uninterrupted effect, impact, and influence, within their assigned domain. What this commandment actually speaks to, then, is the law of the *longevity* of tradition in the *domain* proper to it.

Tradition

Tradition is the moral content of time in the same way that rightful retribution is the moral content of causality. Things following one after another, conceived merely as succession (that is, purely as time), remain inessential and morally hollow if they are not joined to the marrow of tradition. Tradition is the moral backbone of time. It is the ever-present vertebration of what came before with what follows after, whether in terms of progress and regression, or of ascent and decline. Culture and civilization are simply other ways of saying "tradition."

Time as Amoral Evolution. Science, however, assigns to time the very different meaning of *development* in the sense of biological evolution, which depends upon two factors: conservation through the law of heredity and so-called mutations that alter the course of heredity (novel factors which from time to time impinge upon otherwise conservative hereditary transmission). The theory of biological evolution, then, presupposes three things: *conservation* through heredity (lacking which, the existence of species would be inconceivable); *mutation* (lacking which, there would be no progress, and thus no evolution); and *time* itself. As understood here, however, time is meant solely as an all-powerful "master teacher"—one that, in the unfolding of empirical experience and random occurrence, assigns incalculable latitude for natural selection, adaptation, and breeding to run their course. And since time in this sense *is* evolution, belief in evolution is tantamount to belief in time.

But in the present case of biological theory, belief in evolution (or belief in time) implies, not higher moral evolution, but survival of the fittest. According to this teaching, what evolution aspires to through its school of trial and error is the capacity to adapt to, or to dominate, the environment. From this point of view, the evolution of humankind does not bring forth saints and sages, but mechanics and engineers instead—for, those equipped with technical competence are far better fitted to the struggle for existence.

Seen in this light, the official Soviet Union promotion of

authors as "engineers of the psyche" amounts to a strategy to translate the role of author into a general scheme of functional utility. Thus the author is redirected from serving truth, goodness, and beauty to cultivating psychological forces that are useful (indeed indispensable) for advancing plans to "quantitatively" stimulate production while at the same time "qualitatively" galvanizing an entire society to commit themselves to such a scheme!

Communists are adherents of evolution in just this sense, and so have no use for truth, goodness, and beauty as ends in themselves. For them, truth is what is useful, good is what is well-adapted, beautiful is what lends a pleasing facade to some utilitarian function. For them, a new railroad being laid in Siberia is no mere construction project; rather, it is to be treated as an article of faith, celebrated in song, daubed on canvas, movingly portrayed in literature as yet another jewel in the crown of communism. In sum, time conceived as evolution is *amoral*, and the consequences of amoral ideas are most often *immoral*.

Time as Living Tradition. We relate to the world very differently when time is not conceived as amoral evolution but as the bearer of living tradition. For in the context of tradition (that is, in the stream of past, present, and future), time is transmuted into a morally-interconnected, organic whole. In this whole, the *past* ("fathers" and "mothers") is honored, valued, and cherished as the inexhaustible source of the living water of tradition flowing into the *future*. And every *present* moment of this temporal stream offers the possibility and the opportunity both to reflect on the values of tradition recalled from the past and to look to the future in hopeful anticipation of its ripening fruits.

From this we can readily understand that another essential aspect of living tradition is its resistance to the powers of forgetting, sleep, and death, for these three are expressions of a single principle, that of *perishing* in the course of time.

Now, general life-experience teaches that time effects a tendency toward forgetting, falling asleep, and death; for every involvement with time—every reliance on time, every compromise with time—opens wide the gate leading inevitably to forgetting, sleep, and death.

The gospel text (Matthew 16:18) concerning the conversation at Caesarea Philippi is usually rendered: "and the gates of *hades* (hell) will not overcome it." However, *hades* (which corresponds to the Hebrew *sheol*) does not mean the place or condition of the *damned*; it means the kingdom of the *dead*—or, simply, *death*. Gates of death, then, are entrances and exits along the stream of time, every one of which leads to death. The pledge in Jesus Christ's words, "You are Peter and on this rock I will build my Church, and the gates of hades will not overcome it" contains the mandate, the promise, and the blessing of freedom from time, which is to say the power to resist the tendencies of death. This mandate, promise, and blessing pledges that, for as long as the Church remains firmly set upon the rock of the See of Peter as a living tradition, it will remain immune to the death-dealing influences of time. Temporal influences will never overcome the Church nor gain the upper hand within the Church for as long as the See of Peter fulfills Christ's pledge to maintain the living tradition—which *is* the Church—and by doing so preserve it from passing away.

⊕

Every living tradition is based upon two forces working together: the sustaining force of *memory* (oriented toward the past) and the force of *hope* (oriented toward the future). The former preserves the past from being forgotten, the latter gives shape to the future as the path toward fulfillment. In other words, the *motherly* principle preserves tradition and the *fatherly* principle guides it toward its future goal. The continuing viability or longevity of tradition (of *every* tradition) is bound up with the commandment "Honor your father and your mother."

The "faculty of memory" upon which the life of tradition depends is no mere recollection of ideas from the past, but the capacity of the soul in all its fullness to bring the past alive *in* the present. So, for example, the devotional practice of the fourteen stations of the Way of the Cross, which according to tradition the most holy Virgin Mother herself introduced, is no mere memory exercise (an effort to recall what happened at that time and in just what order), but a striving to experience *as present* what is unforgettable about Christ's way to his crucifixion.

Furthermore, Christ's last words at the institution of the holy sacrament at the Last Supper, "Do this in memory of me," attest that all the sacraments of the Church are *revivifications* in the present of what took place in the past. In the holy sacrament at the altar, for example, remembrance becomes the divine-magical act of transubstantiation, an act relating to the *real*, not merely the *recalled*, presence of the body and blood of the Redeemer. In the divine-magical act of transubstantiation, what took place before (at the institution of the sacrament of the altar at the Last Supper) takes place again now, in the present.

In a sacrament, memory does not travel back into the past, but summons the past into the present, evoking something from the realm of forgetting, sleep, and death. Such memory as this may come to bear the same power that sounded forth in the call of the Master, "Lazarus, come forth!"—a call, let us not forget, that proved equal to its task. In this way, memory becomes divine magic. It becomes a miracle of great love and faith. In truth, the words "Do this in memory of me" actually mean "Do this, so that I may be *present.*"

And need we add that the Son of Man is also *Lord over time?*

⊕

Tradition could not remain viable for long, however, solely on the strength of the sustaining and revivifying power of remembrance of the past. To remain viable, it requires will that is directed at *perfecting* the tradition, at *shaping* the future. Such a will revealed itself concretely in figures like St. Augustine and St. Ignatius of Loyola (and perhaps in all founders of orders). With utmost loyalty and devotion, St. Augustine held fast to what Mother Church treasured in *memory* of the past, and also to her *authority,* which he considered highest and most decisive. But he also depicted the great future *goal* of the Church and of the universal spiritual history of humankind in his work *De Civitate Dei* (*The City of God*), which laid a foundation for the history of philosophy as well. As for St. Ignatius, he established an order and a method of instruction directed at educating others to become worthy contenders in the quest to bring Augustine's "City of God" to realization. (As is well known, the rules of the Augustinian order were adopted as the basis for the life and activity of the "Society of Jesus"—which was founded many centuries later by St. Ignatius.)

What do the rules of a spiritual order amount to? They express the *will* of its founder, the "father" of the order (to whom his "sons" freely pledge obedience), which is oriented toward a *goal*, toward an *ideal*. By fulfilling the will of their "father"—that is, by taking the rules as the content of their own will—they "honor their father." This, then, is the other side of the secret of the longevity of tradition as expressed more fully in the commandment: "Honor your father and your mother, that your days may be long in the land that the Lord your God gives you."

It is a fact that the religious orders of the Catholic Church[4] reveal an astonishing longevity, surpassed only by that of the Church itself. What is the secret of this longevity, the secret of the "days that may be long" of the religious communal orders? It is that they are *faithful* to the Church as their "mother," and that they strive to *fulfill the will* of their founders, their "fathers," in accordance with their vows. The secret of their longevity lies in fulfilling the commandment: "Honor your father and your mother."

[4] The Orthodox Church does not, properly speaking, have religious orders, but instead has individual monastic communities that to a greater or lesser extent continue the tradition of the Cenobite communities of the Desert Fathers. AUTHOR

THE
SIXTH
COMMANDMENT

"You Shall Not Kill"
Exodus 20:13

The Prohibition of Destruction

HILE THE FIFTH COMMANDMENT, "HONOR YOUR father and your mother," portrays the foundation for the longevity of tradition, it implies also a prohibition against destroying the continuity of life—not just of physical life based on heredity but also of the life of tradition, understood as the *moral-spiritual content* of the passage of time.[1] Time is implicitly a process

---

[1] In the original text, this chapter begins by pointing out that the seventh, eighth, ninth, and tenth commandments (those prohibiting adultery, stealing, slander, and coveting the neighbors' possessions) are all contained in the sixth commandment; i.e, that they are all "particular applications" of the prohibition against killing. These latter are then briefly considered (in reverse order) before resuming a detailed consideration of the sixth commandment. Since, up till now, a separate chapter has been devoted to each commandment, we have taken the liberty of repositioning the final four commandments to two following chapters: the first on the seventh commandment, and the second on the final three commandments (preserving the author's reverse sequence of these three).

111

of depreciation, degeneration, sclerosis: in a word, *death*. In contrast, tradition is the sustaining power of *life* that counters the "gates of hades" (death). To trace one's blood-line through a long-standing family (in the sense of heredity) has positive value only if the family line concerned is the bearer of a living moral-spiritual tradition; for in fact, being a scion of an "old family" generally speaking carries with it a degree of physical and spiritual degeneration. A case in point is that of the descendants of Crusaders who betrayed the original ideals and duties of Christian knighthood and fell into brigandry. Almost inevitably the reward for betraying tradition is degeneration in the family hereditary line— to the point of debilitation and weakmindedness.

Tradition is *ensouled time*. Life is *ensouled corporality*. To kill, then, is to "un-ensoul" corporality, to separate soul from body. But the sixth commandment, "You shall not kill," forbids not only the violent separation by murder of another's soul from his body; but equally so, it forbids the violent *un*-ensouling of tradition, whose continuance of life is founded upon honoring father and mother. Such "murder" of tradition takes place on a grand scale, and no less frequently than the murder of individuals.

When, for example, Christian missionaries do not undertake to convert so-called "natives" by allowing the unique moral beauty and spiritual richness of Christianity to speak for itself, but instead by persuading them that their fathers and mothers were in error (e.g., for worshipping the sun, moon, and stars as divine and passing this worship on to their descendents), they are engaged in murder. By thus *un*-ensouling a living tradition, they effectively teach: "Do *not* honor your father and your mother."

This was a moral problem that troubled Francis Xavier,

concerning which he sought advice in a letter to the General of the Jesuit Order, St. Ignatius. In that letter, he described the deep loyalty of the natives (whose conversion to Christianity he was concerned with) to the commandment: "Honor your father and your mother." They made clear to him (so he wrote) that if the fate of the unbaptized is the place of damnation, and the fate of the baptized is the blessedness of heaven, they preferred to share the fate of their fathers and their mothers in the place of damnation rather than win divine blessedness for themselves in heaven at the cost of abandoning their fathers and mothers. "What is one to do or say in response to this?" asked Francis Xavier of St. Ignatius.

Other missionaries, less sensitive than Francis Xavier, simply took for granted that the religion of the indigenous peoples whom they sought to convert was the work of the devil, and acted accordingly: they sowed doubt and mistrust among their would-be converts, and through disdain for their "fathers and mothers" killed off their living tradition to commandeer room for a new one. Their attitude was: "Kill to make room for new life."

This, however, was *not* the attitude of the very first missionary, the apostle Paul! In his missionary journeys, Paul established rapport with the most valuable elements of the living traditions he encountered along the way, and took pains to explain to their adherents how these elements had now reached their perfection and fulfillment in the Christian message. In this respect he was both a "Jew among the Jews" and a "Greek among the Greeks." When among the Greeks, he did not approach the Athenian altar erected to "the unknown God" as a work of the devil. When among the Jews, he did not deny their messianic expectation, but approached it from the standpoint that this expectation was now fulfilled in Jesus Christ.

Unfortunately, as time moved on, Paul's approach was abandoned as the *modus operandi* of the Church's missionary activity. Destruction and compulsion were brought to bear in its stead, especially during the time when triumphal Christianity became the state religion of the Roman Empire (approximately from the time of Constantine the Great to that of Justinian). As a first step in this process, the official practice of the old religious cults was forbidden. Then temples and other ritual sites serving these cults were desecrated and shut down. Then, even private devotion to the former cults was forbidden under pain of death. Finally, by abolishing the Academy in Athens and banishing its teachers from the Empire, Justinian put an end even to the tradition of Hellenistic philosophy.

In order to make place for the life of the newer tradition, the religious-cultic life and the philosophical tradition of the Hellenes were expunged. Thus did triumphal Christianity, as state religion of the Roman Empire, kill off the "fathers and mothers" of the former pagan traditions—a deed that differed in no essential respect from what, in its turn, the ruling pagan state religion of the Roman Empire had earlier perpetrated in its efforts to suffocate the emergent, living tradition of Christianity.

But the *essence* of something living cannot be destroyed; its *soul* persists. When either an individual soul or the soul of a tradition is separated from its bodily vehicle, its essence retreats into a condition outside the frame of consciousness. There it remains active, and sooner or later it will reveal itself again in a conscious state. Initially it lives on as a latent inclination, a yearning, to incorporate itself again

in the form of a clear, conscious disposition and orientation. Then a "renaissance" takes place: a rebirth of the spirit
of the individual or of the tradition that had outwardly
been repressed and, to all appearances, had been stifled.
Then the former love toward the primal ancestral fathers
and mothers that had seemed to fade away (forgotten,
fallen asleep, overcome) returns to life, together with the
tradition which the primal fathers and mothers concerned
had represented, and for which that people and that tradition had lived.

The commandment "You shall not kill" expresses an
absolute truth, for it is in fact not possible, in the spiritual
realm, to kill anything living. In truth, in a deeper sense,
there is no such thing as killing. What actually takes place in
the process so often misconstrued as death is not extinction
but "inner transformation," an alchemical process of *interiorization*. In this sense, it can be said that no ideal or idea
from the past that was ever embraced with serious conviction (not excepting even ideals or ideas later found to have
been mistaken) ever truly dies. Even heresies do not die:
they emerge over and over again, regardless of whether they
are believed to have long since perished. The same holds
true in the broad domain of pre-Christian paganism, by
which we mean "belief in the cosmos." We find today's version of this paganism in the belief in the widespread tribute
paid to the "all-encompassing evolution" which dominates
our educational and cultural life in precisely the same way
that the "cosmic myths" of pagan antiquity dominated the
educational and cultural life of pre-Christian times.

The measures taken by the pagan Caesars to suppress or
kill off Christianity as a living tradition led, in the end, to
Christian domination over the Roman world. But then the

measures taken in their turn by later Christian Caesars to suppress or kill off paganism (by likewise persecuting its adherents and thoroughly eradicating it) led ultimately to the reconquest of paganism over Christianity in the form of "belief in the cosmos." The only real difference this time was that "belief in the cosmos" appeared now in the guise of "belief in evolution"—a belief now pervasively embedded as an undeniable fact of life throughout the "global empire" of so-called Western Christian civilization!

⊕

The teaching of world history under consideration here is unmistakable: "You shall not kill." This lesson *must* be learned, for in the final analysis, there is no other way to overcome error than alchemical transformation by means of interiorization, ennoblement, and contemplation. This transformative process leads, through tolerance and peaceful coexistence, to inner deepening. But it leads to this same inner deepening also through direct-but-tolerant confrontation between error and truth, between the merely useful and the good, between the merely imposing and noble beauty.

By open confrontation under conditions of tolerance, we do *not* mean, however, submersion and, finally, drowning in the *relativism* of the Pilate-question: "What is truth?" Rather, we mean confrontation between truths and values that, although absolute, *do not engender a desire to suppress or kill*. The tolerance we have in mind should reflect God's tolerance as portrayed in this Jewish legend:

> While Abraham was on one of his journeys, he
> wanted to set up his tent for the night to rest. Sud-
> denly, a lonely wanderer appeared and requested his

hospitality. Abraham granted his hospitality, and shared his evening meal with him. After the meal, Abraham suggested to the stranger that they pray together. Then, to Abraham's dismay and indignation, it became apparent that the stranger was a pagan, and in fact a fire-worshipper. Filled with anger, Abraham wanted to kill him. Then the Lord appeared to Abraham in a vision and commanded him not to do this. The Lord spoke: "Abraham! I have tolerated this man for fifty years, and you will not tolerate him for even one night?" And Abraham was ashamed and allowed the stranger to spend the night in his tent.

This does not mean that, in standing by his original offer of hospitality, Abraham was *ipso facto* acknowledging the "relative truth" of fire-worship, and thereby relativizing his *own* belief in the one and only God! Rather, Abraham came to see that in our dealings with each other we ought to take as our model *God's patience.* Tolerance is not a relativizing indifference! No, it is a patience that does not begrudge others the time and the opportunity they may require along their own path of continuing interiorization and contemplation in order to come to deeper insight. The rock, the See of St. Peter, is not only rock-solid *belief* in face of unavoidable encounters and confrontations with different spiritual streams over the course of time. It is also a rock-solid *patience* that bears within it the "certainty" of *faith.*

⊕

Through the centuries, the combination of an unyielding, unshakable firmness of faith with *abiding patience* has rendered the rock of the See of St. Peter invincible against whatever conflicts have been sent against it; for all such conflicts ultimately amount to no more than passing winds and waves. Every "demand of the times" is necessarily ephemeral. Equally ephemeral, for the same reason, are all efforts to "democratize" the Church, to "de-dogmatize" the teachings of the Church on the pretense that psychological interpretations and other such proposals are fit to "modernize" the Church, her teachings, and her standards. For all these demands, without exception, offend against the commandment "Honor your father and your mother" and open wide the gates of the path leading to death (*hades*). May the emulators of innovations among theologians and laity alike consider for once their full responsibility in light of the commandment "You shall not kill."

The life and death of a living tradition is analogous to the life and death of an individual, for even as the life of an individual is his ensouled *corporality*, so is the life of a tradition its ensouled *corpus* of transmitted teaching. Divesting the ensouled corporality of an individual of his soul means death for that individual, even as divesting a tradition of the ensouled corpus of its transmitted teaching spells death for that tradition.

THE
SEVENTH
COMMANDMENT

"You Shall Not Commit Adultery"
Exodus 20:14

Adultery as a Form of Killing

HAT MYSTERIOUS POWER BINDS SOUL TO BODY? It is no mere contract, and it is deeper than symbiotic interdependence. In truth, soul and body *yearn* for one another: the soul yearns to be enveloped in the blood's warmth; the body yearns for the stimulation it receives when it is fully ensouled. It is the power of mutual *love* that unites soul and body. Life, which is the union of soul and body, is their *marriage* also. This is why the seventh commandment, "You shall not commit adultery," comes after the sixth: "You shall not kill." Adultery is a kind of killing because it violates marriage, which is the very archetype of the union of soul and body!

The notion that marriage is analogous to the union of soul and body can be traced through the books of the Old Testament like a scarlet thread. Furthermore, Jewish tradition regards the covenant of the community of Israel with YHVH as deeper than a mere contract—in fact, it regards this covenant as a marriage. In the prophetic books of the

Bible, infidelity toward the God who revealed Himself on Mt. Sinai (i.e., "rebellion" against His worship in favor of worship of Baal and Astaroth) is accordingly called "adultery and fornication." Among all others in the world, the community of Israel was chosen as "bride and spouse" of the LORD their God "who is a jealous God and does not tolerate other gods before him." The community of Israel did not choose YHVH as their Lord and God: YHVH chose *them*! When the community of Israel was chosen as bride of the invisible and unimaginable God YHVH, an eternal covenant was entered into that demanded eternal loyalty: on the part of Israel, in the form of exclusive reverence and obedience toward the invisible Bridegroom; on the part of God, in the form of His eternal, guiding presence in Israel's destiny.

For this reason, the Ark of the Covenant (and later, Solomon's Temple) was the place where the meeting with the Omnipresent One could be experienced, where the splendor (*shekinah*) of God filled the Holy of Holies. This splendor, or radiating presence, of God was not an idea, still less a theological or poetic trope, but a reality that could no less deal out death than life. It was so real that to touch the Ark of the Covenant in the absence of proper authority meant instant death.

⊕

The gravity of the covenant between YHVH and Israel can be seen in the book of Job. Overcome by the unwonted degree of Job's suffering during his trials, his wife advised him: "Renounce YHVH and *die!*" (Job 2:9) Desperate though it was, this counsel clearly illustrates that the covenant of the community of Israel with YHVH was as gravely real as life and death. It was in all essentials equivalent to the bond between an individual's soul and body, which if dissolved means, quite precisely, death. YHVH's covenant with Israel was no mere contract of mutual expedience; it was, rather, an indissoluble union of soul and body: YHVH as soul and the community of Israel as body.

The covenant between YHVH-ELOHIM and the community of Israel was also a bond of marriage. It was a true marriage in the sense that all fathers of the people of Israel begat children in the name of YHVH, out of His impulse and for His future purposes; and all mothers of the people of Israel bore their children as a gift and blessing of the God of Israel. The mothers conceived, carried to term, and bore their children as parts and members of *one* mother: the community of Israel. And as the sign that procreation was not just an individual affair, but that the power of YHVH played a part in it, at His behest *circumcision* of the male representatives of the people of Israel was made an obligatory religious practice. Procreation and the multiplying of the people was the preserve of YHVH. And beyond this, He would also care for future generations, for the children and the children's children. YHVH-ELOHIM was LORD over the destiny of the future generations of the chosen people, *His* people.

Thus the seventh commandment, "You shall not commit adultery," contains a powerful, even suprahuman, behest: just as the Holy One of Israel is faithful to the covenant with Israel, so is the community of Israel to remain faithful to its LORD. Furthermore, the marriage covenant of YHVH with the people of Israel is mirrored in the marriage bond between man and woman. This is why the violation of fidelity toward their God "before Whom you shall have no other gods" on the part of the Israelite community was viewed as an adulterous mirror-image of fidelity to the marriage bond. Since the sixth commandment, "You shall not kill," mandates the obligation to remain faithful to the bond uniting soul to body, and since (*mutatis mutandis*) this bond is likewise that of marriage, severing this bond through adultery is *also* a form of murder. *Murder and adultery go hand in hand.*

In truth,[1] the seventh, eighth, ninth, and tenth commandments—those prohibiting adultery, stealing, slander, and coveting the neighbors' possessions—are *all* contained in the sixth commandment: "You shall not kill." They are all particular applications of the prohibition against killing, against severing the bond that holds body and soul together.

---

[1] As indicated on page III, fn I (regarding the sixth commandment).

THE
FINAL THREE
COMMANDMENTS

*Coveting, Giving False Testimony, and
Stealing—All as Forms of Killing*

[E HAVE SEEN THAT THE SEVENTH COMMAND-
ment, "You shall not commit adultery," is contained in the sixth, "You shall not kill"; and
furthermore, that the final three command-
ments are *also* particular applications of the prohibition
against killing—understood here in its more general sense
of severing the bond that holds body and soul together, as
the author briefly summarizes in reverse order.] ED.

The Tenth Commandment. "You shall not covet the possessions of your neighbor." In this case, let us consider the fact
that the primary, immediate sphere of action for our consciousness is our own body. We may say that the body is the
soul's most intimate "possession," that the body is that portion of the outside world which *belongs* more to the soul
than does anything else of that world. The possessive nature
of this affiliation can get so tight a hold on us and be so intimate that our soul may even come to *identify* itself with the
body, in which case the soul will characterize and perceive
the body as its very self or "I." This identification can go

123

very far indeed, so far that we often hear it said that "the human being *has* a soul." In this expression, "the human being" is clearly being taken to mean the body! But it would be more correct to put it the other way around: "the human being (as soul) has a body"! For it is our body that our soul *has*. That is, the body is the soul's *possession*. The truth of it is that we *are* our soul, and that our soul possesses the body as its own immediate sphere of action. Now, if our body is that portion of the outside world which is in the special, intimate possession of our soul, so, *mutatis mutandis*, we may also regard as our own possession in this sense whatever further portions of the outside world may have come "into our possession" as our soul's "extended" sphere of action.

In the sense of the tenth commandment, then, we may say for example that the neighbor's house, yard, garden, and fields (as further bodily extensions of *his* soul) are to be counted among the "neighbor's possessions" that we are commanded not to covet.

The Ninth Commandment. "You shall not give false testimony against your neighbor." Now, just as bodily extensions of the soul may be pictured as its "possession" (i.e., as part of its "extended body") in the sense of the tenth commandment, so may the good reputation, respect, and trust a neighbor soul enjoys in converse with others be represented as that neighbor's "extended soul." Here it is a matter of how one "extended soul" *projects* itself into that of its neighbor—that is, how the former, having thus impinged upon and thereby been reflected within the latter, may *affect* it. This brings us to the heart of the ninth commandment. For, if extended into the neighbor's soul, such transgressions as slander ("false testimony") may work in a withering, distorting, destructive way upon that neighbor's soul. False testimony is in effect *moral* murder.

The Eighth Commandment. "You shall not steal." Without developing the point further here, we may say (in conformity with the line of thought offered above) that the transgression of the "extended soul" of one who steals from his neighbor is tantamount not only to moral murder, but to moral *theft* as well.

⊕

The interdictions represented by the final four commandments follow from the fact that the giver of the ten commandments is the God of life, of joining together and uniting—and *not* of death, of separating body from soul, of separating man from woman, of separating possession from possessor.

The final four commandments, as we have said, are all contained in the sixth commandment, "You shall not kill." We have also shown that the sixth commandment is in turn an extension of the fifth commandment, regarding the longevity of tradition: "Honor your father and your mother." They have to do with life, marriage, possession, and honor —honor, that is, toward the soul of the other, the neighbor. *The life, marriage, possessions, and honor of another are just as inviolable as are our own.*

⊕

Now, the fifth commandment, to "honor your father and your mother," is related in turn to the fourth commandment, to "keep the sabbath holy," that is, to the absolute necessity for the soul to reserve periods of quiet for the sake of interiorization in order to keep alive the bond between God and the human "I." For it is this interiorization in peace and quiet that enables us to become aware of the father-love and mother-love of the fifth commandment as mirrors of Divine Love.

⊕

The ten commandments are a reflection of the splendor of the world-order. They are an expression of *truth* that is, as it were, crystallized in them.[1] [In pursuance of the above line of contemplation, we may ask what is the relationship of the fourth commandment, "to keep the sabbath holy," to the first, second, and third commandments. Here, then, we complete our course through the ten commandments by sketching out what constitutes their essential nature.]

First Commandment ("You shall have *no other* gods before me"): Just as the multivalence of the soul's life of imagination, feeling, and will has a central focus around which it orders and orients itself, so too does the peripheral multiplicity of cosmic manifestation as a whole have *one* central focus that orders and holds everything together. And just as the human self is the centerpoint of the plurality of the soul's manifestations, so is the *one* God-above-the-self the centerpoint of the world.

---

[1] Since the text here is so condensed in the original, some bracketed text, parenthetical citations of relevant commandments, and subheadings have been introduced to highlight the author's final formulations regarding the union, through love, of man and God. This material stands at the end of the final chapter in the original; but it summarizes the overall presentation of the ten commandments so succinctly that it seemed fitting to place it here, before moving on to the question "Who is Yahweh?"

Second Commandment ("You shall not make for yourself an *image*... for I, the LORD your God, am a jealous god... but showing *love* to a thousand generations of those who *love* me and keep my commandments"): The plurality of cosmic manifestation may be likened to a periphery; and its unity may be likened to the *center* of that periphery. Now, that center—which holds together the periphery of multiform cosmic manifestation, giving it meaning and direction—is no other than the very Self of the cosmos. And as for that peripheral multiplicity of cosmic manifestation, it can form no *image* of the God-above-the-self.

Third Commandment ("You shall not misuse the *name* of the LORD your God"): Neither can the peripheral multiplicity of cosmic manifestation proclaim His *name*. For the *unimaginable* and *unnameable* God-above-the-self can *only* be recognized and named in the language of the self. But the self's own language is that of *love*. The human self speaks only *in* love and *through* love; otherwise it remains silent. Love is the life-element of the soul, its substance, its power of growth. Love is also the source of certainty concerning God's presence in the world, for it is the bond of love that unites the self with God. Love recognizes God, just as the human self is recognized *by* God.

⊕

Here we touch upon the union of Man and God through love, which in turn raises the fundamental question: Who exactly is this God—YHVH? To this question we now turn.

WHO IS YHVH?

S WE DRAW THESE CONSIDERATIONS TO A CLOSE, we have to ask: Who is YHVH-ELOHIM? Who is the Revealer on Mt. Sinai? Who is the Partner of the covenant with Israel? Is the Godhead of the world—is the Creator, Redeemer, and Interiorizor of the world; or again, is the eternal Holy Trinity of Father, Son, and Holy Spirit—identical with YHVH, the LORD of the community of Israel? The answer is: yes and no. This contradiction can be resolved by way of synthesis if we recall that, in essence, the religion of Israel was and remains a *prophetic* religion, a religion founded upon the revelation of the prophets. But first we must distinguish between two kinds of prophet: *proclaimers*, such as Isaiah and Jeremiah; and *wonder-workers*, such as Elijah and Elisha.

The proclaiming prophets did not speak out of themselves, but from and in the name of the God-above-the-self, to Whom they offered their very selves. These prophets became mouthpieces of God. Similarly, the wonder-working prophets became instruments for the operations of God's magical power, which surrounded and filled them. They emptied themselves of their personal will in order to become such instruments of divine power. For his part, Moses was *both* proclaimer and wonder-worker; whereas Elijah, above all, bore divine-magical power: he was a wonder-worker, not a seer.

Now, Scripture teaches that prophetic missions are not limited to humankind, but that they extend as well to

129

beings of the spiritual hierarchies, often called "angels" for short. Thus, the first meeting of Moses with God took place when, in the vicinity of Mt. Horeb in the land of Midian, He revealed Himself to Moses by calling to him through the intercession of an angel:

> And the angel of the LORD appeared to him in a flame of fire out of the midst of a bush. . . . When the LORD saw that he turned aside to see, God called to him out of the bush: "Moses, Moses!" (Exodus 3:2–4)

The angel of the LORD was in the burning bush, and through that angel God called out: "Moses, Moses!" When that angel called Moses by name, it did so as hierarchical bearer and emissary of the LORD. This was the same angel through whom, somewhat earlier (when assigning Moses the task of leading the people of Israel out of Egypt) God made Himself known as the God of Abraham, Isaac, and Jacob. When proclaiming from the burning bush, then, the angel of the LORD spoke and acted in a manner similar to that of human prophets, who likewise speak and act, not from themselves, but from the Being of God-above-the-self Who fills and rules them.

The notion of revelation from the Most High through human and hierarchical beings is well known to tradition, as also to iconography. Thus, the Rublev icon depicting the three angels whom Abraham welcomed and fed is considered to be in fact an icon of the Holy Trinity (even though it actually depicts three angelic beings sitting at table) because there is no doubt that the Holy Trinity is revealing itself through the three angels. Clearly, the icon's message is that Abraham's meeting was not merely with the three angels, but with the Trinity.

Looked at this way (which is quite in keeping with Christian tradition), we must answer in the affirmative the question whether the God of Abraham, Isaac, and Jacob (who also revealed Himself to Moses near Mt. Horeb) is the same as the trinitarian God of Christianity. But looked at another way—taking into consideration especially the role Scripture grants prophets and hierarchical beings as representatives of the Divine—the angel of the LORD (to take one example) who spoke from the burning bush *in the name of* the God of Abraham, Isaac, and Jacob was clearly *just* an angel and *not* the God of Abraham, Isaac, and Jacob Himself.

Just as Moses's mission to lead the people of Israel out of Egypt was proclaimed from the burning bush by an angelic being, so did another hierarchical being—delegated to this task by the Most High—proclaim the ten commandments to Moses from the dark cloud amid flashes of lightning and peals of thunder. And it was *this* hierarchical being Who entered into the covenant with the people of Israel in the name, and on behalf of, the Most Holy One.

⊕

YHVH-ELOHIM exhibits individual features characteristic of hierarchical beings, just as Elijah (to take one example) exhibits individual features characteristic of human beings. For even though their missions are divine, both wonder-working and proclaiming "prophets" (whether human or hierarchical beings) exhibit an *individual* character. When Moses shattered the stone tablets, this was no part of fulfilling his prophetic mission of proclaiming the ten commandments, but solely an expression of his individual indignation at the revolt staged at the foot of Mt. Sinai by those worshipping the golden calf. Similarly, such biblical descriptions of YHVH-ELOHIM's actions as His punishing decrees as the "jealous God" (imposed out of anger, and later revoked) show that, in fulfilling the task set Him by the eternal Holy Trinity, YHVH-ELOHIM nonetheless had leeway to express His individual nature.

Indeed, the particular features of YHVH-ELOHIM's individual nature, as depicted in the Bible, even suggest to which rank of the spiritual hierarchies He belongs. That rank is made plain in the biblical episodes of His characteristic mode of action: demonstrating His *power*. We see this first in the transformation of the rod of Moses into a snake that swallows the snakes created by the Egyptian priests in a similar manner. Next come the ten plagues inflicted upon Egypt, and then the destruction of Pharaoh's army in the Red Sea. Clearly, the argument that should have convinced Pharaoh and the Egyptians to let the Israelites go was that they had on their side a mighty, invisible ally who wielded such power over the elements that it was senseless to resist His will!

⊕

The traditional Church teaching on the celestial or angelic hierarchies as found in Paul's writings was later presented in minute detail by Dionysius the Areopagite in his work *Concerning the Heavenly Hierarchy*. Many centuries later, this teaching (as transmitted by Dionysius) was elaborated in a most intellectually satisfying way by St. Thomas Aquinas in his tract on the angels in his *Summa Theologiae*. His contemporary, St. Bonaventure, made use of this same teaching as a contemplative practice on the path of interior enlightenment in his work *Concerning the Threefold Path*. According to St. Bonaventure's teaching, the heavenly choir is made up of three hierarchical levels, each further divided into three orders or ranks. The ranks of the lowest hierarchy (the first hierarchy, as viewed from our perspective) are the angels (*angeloi*), archangels (*archangeloi*), and principalities (*archai*). The ranks of the second hierarchy are the powers (*exusiai*), virtues (*dynameis*), and dominions (*kyriotetes*). The ranks of the third hierarchy, the highest (again, as viewed from our perspective) are the thrones (*thronoi*), cherubim (*cherubim*), and seraphim (*seraphim*). St. Bonaventure elucidates the role that these nine ranks of the heavenly choir play in the meditative comprehension of truth as follows:

> Note that, in the first hierarchy, truth is to be *invoked* by sighing and prayer (work of the *angels*); to be *heard* and *received* by study and reading (work of the *archangels*); to be *proclaimed* by example and preaching (work of the *principalities*).
>
> In the second hierarchy we *come closer* to the truth by taking refuge in it and devoting ourselves to it (work of the *powers*); we come to *grasp* it through eagerness and emulation (work of the *virtues*); we *enter into covenant* with it by self-abnegation and dying to self (work of the *dominions*).
>
> In the third hierarchy, truth is to be *venerated* by sacrifice and praise (work of the *thrones*); to be *wondered at* through ecstasy and contemplation (work of the *cherubim*); to be embraced with loving caress (work of the *seraphim*).[1]

---

[1] *De triplici via*, III, §7, 14 (*Opera Omnia* 8, 18), author's translation. See also *The Works of St. Bonaventure*, vol. 1, *Mystical Opuscula*, trans. José de Vinck (Patterson, NJ: Sr. Anthony Guild Press, 1960), 93–94.

St. Bonaventure closes this text with the words: "Note these things carefully, for they hold the fountain of life." We wholeheartedly agree with this advice, for this text truly does contain a fountain of spiritual life!

⊕

The teaching on the heavenly hierarchies was renewed in the first quarter of the twentieth century by the great Austrian seer and thinker Rudolf Steiner. The depth and breadth of Steiner's contribution to a new understanding of the spiritual hierarchies is such that this theme cannot be seriously considered today without taking into account his remarkable achievement, which, in regard to wealth of stimulation, depth and multiplicity of viewpoints, inner lack of contradiction, and organic cohesion, is not to be compared with any seer or thinker—whether of the present, of the middle ages, or of antiquity—for it towers above them all!

Steiner viewed the spiritual hierarchies as holding sway throughout the unfolding of our world and its history. In his writings and lecture cycles (for example, *An Outline of Esoteric Science* and *Spiritual Beings in the Heavenly Bodies and in the Kingdoms of Nature*) he offered a comprehensive description of the nature and role of the spiritual hierarchies, both in the primal establishment of the cosmic order and in its subsequent and ongoing unfolding. Indeed, it can be said that, throughout his literary and lecturing activity, Steiner held the heavenly hierarchies constantly in view and strove unremittingly to do full justice to their reality. He laid up a "thought-cathedral" in homage to the hierarchies—and this in the twentieth century, when knowledge concerning their reality had virtually disappeared! Take whatever position you like regarding his theses and viewpoints on the hierarchical world order—but all must concede that Steiner rendered an inestimable service by making comprehensible again, in a renewed and revitalized form, the nature and the role of angels, archangels, archai, exusiai, dynameis, kyriotetes, thrones, cherubim, and seraphim. These choirs of higher beings were retrieved from the realm of forgetting, sleep, and death—recalled to memory, reawakened, and resurrected—in and through Steiner's lifework. The first duty of anyone who may henceforward undertake to rationalize or "psychologize" away the reality of the spiritual hierarchies must be to grapple with Rudolf Steiner's teaching on this subject.

Furthermore, Steiner's teaching on the angelic hierarchies powerfully *corroborates* the Church's own teaching in their regard—a teaching that for Catholic and Orthodox Christians alike forms an indispensable part of their faith. Should Rudolf Steiner be subjected to criticism solely because his belief in the angelic hierarchies proved so astonishingly fruitful and intellectually enriching? Should he be calumniated solely because his belief in them grew into an actual "spiritual beholding"? If we should choose to disparage him on this account, would we not by implication be tacitly professing that sterile and impoverished thinking are intrinsic to the very nature of belief? But such was not the teaching of the Church at the time of the Church Fathers, nor can it be today! No, the question of which rank of the spiritual hierarchies YHVH-ELOHIM belongs to *obliges* us to take into account Steiner's teaching concerning them.

One feature in Steiner's teaching on the hierarchies is that, although he kept the traditional names for the lowest hierarchy (angels, archangels, archai), he applied to the ranks of the second hierarchy (powers, virtues, dominions) the names "spirits of form," "spirits of movement," and "spirits of wisdom"; and likewise to the ranks of the highest hierarchy (thrones, cherubim, seraphim) the names "spirits of will," "spirits of harmony," and "spirits of love." And it must be said that these names prove to carry just as much meaning as do the traditional names going back to Diony-sius the Areopagite.[2]

⊕

With all this said, let us reframe our question: When YHVH-ELOHIM became the special God of the commu-nity of Israel and, so to say, entered into a marriage covenant with that community as a fully-empowered hierarchical rep-resentative of the eternal Holy Trinity—when He acted, that is, as proclaiming and wonder-working "hierarchical" prophet of the Holy Trinity—to which of the nine ranks of the choir of spiritual hierarchies did He belong?

We have already emphasized that YHVH's *modus oper-andi* during the captivity of the people of Israel in Egypt, as well as during their exodus out of Egypt, is characterized in the Bible as the manifestation of *power*, a power extending

---

[2] In the numbering of the three ranks as quoted from St. Bonaven-ture, care was taken to parenthetically remark that, in his teaching, "first" refers to the hierarchical rank closest to man (angels, archangeloi, archai), and "third" to the rank furthest above man (thrones, cherubim, seraphim). However, in Steiner's work, and in many other teachings on the subject, "first" refers to the highest and "third" to the lowest hierar-chy. Readers who may turn to Steiner's works on this subject will need to bear in mind that what for Bonaventure is the first hierarchy, for Steiner is the third; and likewise, what for Bonaventure is the third hierarchy, is for Steiner the first.

all the way to the elements of nature. This fact alone indicates that YHVH is not a being of the lowest hierarchy (angels, archangels, and archai), because their field of activity is the role of conscience. We need only consider the biblical accounts to discover that no effect on Pharaoh's conscience, or on the conscience of the Egyptian people, was ever attributed to YHVH; and similarly, that the empowering factor for the exodus of the Israelites out of Egypt had nothing whatsoever to do with kindling Pharaoh's conscience to let them go, or with inspiring the Egyptians' insight into the Israelite people's right to leave Egypt. No, what in fact enabled the exodus were the ten plagues inflicted upon the land, and the destruction of the Egyptian army in the waters of the Red Sea.

In other words, the exodus of the people of Israel was made possible by nothing other than the manifestation of YHVH's power over the elements of nature. Now, from the fact that the hierarchical rank of the *powers* or *exusiai* (of the second hierarchy) rules the elements of nature, and is as well (when so authorized from above) empowered to influence natural events, it follows that YHVH—as the fully empowered hierarchical representative, proclaimer, and wonder-working "prophet" of the Most High, is a being of the second hierarchy belonging in fact to the rank of the powers (*exusiai*).[3] It was, then, a being of this rank Who, as God's representative, entered into the special covenantal relationship with the community of Israel and became the providential leader and architect of its path of destiny.

---

[3] Or, according to Steiner's terminology, "spirits of form" (Hebrew: *elohim*). AUTHOR

PROCLAMATION ON SINAI

⊕

Truly, the ten commandments are *in toto* a reflection of the splendor of the cosmic world-order. They are an expression of *truth*, which is, as it were, crystallized in them.

AFTERWORD
On Divine Law

Michael Frensch

I N A LETTER TO HIS CLOSE FRIEND ERNST VON Hippel of June 20, 1970, Tomberg mentions that he has begun writing a text on Moses's ascent of Mt. Sinai and the ten commandments:

> The "ascent of Sinai" is hard work—like all ascents.
> But there is no longer any threat of "going batty."
> That has been overcome.

On April 22, 1971, he speaks of his plan in another letter to his friend:

> I am only writing now to tell you that we are alive, that I continually think of you, that I am making good progress with my study of the ten commandments, and that I hope to finish it in June. Take care. Enjoy life.
>
> Your Valentin, embracing you and Gertrud

On May 20, Tomberg was able once again to report excellent progress to his friend:

> The dark clouds that covered Mt. Sinai, and whose precipitation is the ten commandments, have for the most part given way to light, and were so to speak "transfigured" in the course of my work on those commandments. The study has stood under the sign of the prayer: *Actiones nostras, Domine, aspirando*

139

*praeveni et adjuvando prosequere, ut cuncta nostra oratio
et operatio a te semper incipiat et per te coepta finiatur.*[1]

On July 23, 1971, von Hippel learns from his friend that he is working on the final pages of the work, but has not yet finished it, owing to visits. On August 3rd, von Hippel sends twenty-three pages of corrections to Tomberg's literary executor. On September 15th, Valentin can at last tell the von Hippels that

> work on the ten commandments is completed. It is
> not a long book, but it is very concentrated.

⊕

Why, after finishing his major work, *Lazarus: The Miracle of Resurrection in World History*, did Tomberg undertake the extreme exertion of the "ascent of Sinai," which, in his own words, brought with it the real threat of "going batty"? Why, towards the end of his life, and after having already included in Letter XI of his *Meditations on the Tarot* an extraordinarily profound series of contemplations on the Decalogue, did he again so intensively concern himself with this theme?

Neither in *Meditations on the Tarot* nor in *Proclamation on Sinai* does Tomberg discuss this question directly; but indirectly the text itself suggests an answer: for, in considering the matter, it begins to dawn on us that this late text *looks back* to the essential themes of the two phases of his life.

---

[1] "Direct, we beg thee, O LORD, our prayers and our actions by thy holy inspirations, and carry them on by thy gracious assistance, so that every work of ours may always begin with thee, and through thee come to completion. Amen."

The first theme, that of the *origin of law* (with which he had been preoccupied from the 1940s into the 1950s), is discussed in this final book as a "path through the wilderness," a path he himself so often had to walk as an émigré.

There follows, then, a return to the second theme, that of *essentialism* as the fundamental path of the soul in its quest for *personal certainty* (a primary theme for Tomberg, especially through the 1950s). But now he approaches this theme from a quite different perspective: that of knowledge as a process of mirroring, considered in tandem with the significance of symbols: the Jewish Kabbalah, the nature of the Church, and the meaning of the papacy are all now considered in a new light, as are also the choirs of the spiritual hierarchies—a lifelong theme for Tomberg—culminating in a restored respect for the lifework of Rudolf Steiner (with which he had been so deeply aligned during the first half of his life).

Finally, the "transfiguration of the dark clouds into light" on Mt. Sinai, as here portrayed, signals Tomberg's renewed immersion in the "chronicle" of the world—above all, in what he elsewhere calls the third, or moral, stage of that chronicle.[2]

We may say, then, that this renewed overview of the essential elements of his "second life"—which began with his arrival in Bad Godesberg in 1944, and was, in his own words, distinguished from his previous life as an anthroposophist as if by a "new incarnation"—was granted him at the end of his life from the higher vantage-point of Mt. Sinai.

In what follows, we single out two of the points just mentioned (the *origin of law*, and *essentialism*) as a way to

---

[2] See *Meditations on the Tarot*, Letter XX, "The Judgment."

offer a glimpse of the method and nature of this text, which did *in fact* turn out to be Tomberg's last book, as he himself had spoken of it—in this way, announcing in advance the distinction he himself drew between the authorial projects of the two halves of his life.

⊕

Right at the beginning of the book, Tomberg refers *repeatedly* to the cloud that covered Mt. Sinai, and out of which Moses brought down the ten commandments:

> Exodus, the second book of Moses, depicts the world-historic event of the revelation and proclamation of the Decalogue, or ten commandments. There we read how a thick cloud covered Mt. Sinai, and thunder and lightning accompanied that proclamation: The people remained at a distance, while Moses approached the "thick darkness where God was." (Exodus 20:21) Afterward, Moses emerged from the darkness of the cloud that covered the mountaintop, descended, and proclaimed the divine commandments to the people in their own language and voice. A cloud heavy with revelation lay over the mountain, and Moses "precipitated" this cloud into the ten proclamations of the Decalogue. These proclamations were the humanly comprehensible and accessible *crystallization* of what had taken place in the "thick darkness where God was." [1]

Tomberg is of the view that the Bible itself contains the key to the understanding of what took place in that cloud; for example, the fourth commandment, "Remember the sabbath day, to keep it holy," corresponds to the seventh day of creation, on which God rested from his labors, blessed them, and on this account sanctified the seventh day. And as he says, what goes for the fourth commandment, goes likewise for the others:

> Here the celestial-divine correspondence underlying the fourth commandment, to hallow the sabbath, is expressly indicated: *the celestial-divine archetype of the seventh day of creation is to be reflected in the earthly-human realm.* Herewith the Bible provides the key to understanding the mystery of the cloud upon the mountain: it contained within it the divine-cosmic correspondences of the ten commandments intended for the earthly-human realm. Figuratively speaking, the ten commandments can be seen as "precipitations" of the corresponding archetypes that were contained within the cloud upon the mountain. [2]

At this juncture, the reader may do well to recall the beginning of the second of the two halves of Tomberg's life, when, as a student of law amid a war-torn Germany condemned to moral destruction, he postulated the *divine origin* of law, and argued for a three-stage genesis of law as follows: (1) eternal law (*lex aeterna*), the nature of God, is received and recognized by the higher hierarchies as divine law (*lex divina*); (2) spiritual beings apportion it to the nature of human beings, mediating it to them as natural law (*lex naturalis*); (3) in their lived reality, human beings shape it in turn into positive law valid for individual cases (*lex humana*).

At that time in his development, Tomberg was not yet able to offer decisive proof that *divine law* really did exist. Why? Because such proof cannot be furnished by strictly scientific means; it can only be asserted as dogma. More-over, since he was unable in his professional field of juris-prudence to speak of the higher spiritual hierarchies as representing the moral world-order, it was impossible for him to show that divine law had entered into human con-sciousness, as well as *how* this occurred. During that period, he could do nothing more than characterize this concep-tion of law and argue in its favor.

Now at the end of his life, however—after wrestling for decades with the manner and the nature of personal cer-tainty in spiritual matters—the moment had come for him to devote himself to the proof that had not earlier been pos-sible for him to furnish scientifically. Now it was possible to

> climb with Moses, in spirit, to the top of Mt. Sinai, and
> enter there into the darkness of the cloud "in which
> God was." Only if we are able to retranslate the
> words chiseled upon the stone tablets into the primal
> language of thunder and lightning in which they were
> first proclaimed, will we ever fully grasp that the ten
> commandments are actually of *divine origin*. [3]

⊕

It was during his years in Mülheim, and in London also, that Tomberg finally let go of his commitment to three-stage law. He did so, because jurisprudence in post-war Germany was following more and more the trajectory of law resting solely upon human morality and social relation-ships—i.e., a law not revealed "from above" but fabricated "below."

Considered in the light of Tomberg's expositions of the decalogue, these two conceptions of law are connected with the fact that humanity

is faced with the choice between two principal orientations: toward empirical *existence*, and toward *essence*
or *being*. Depending on how we choose, we become
either an *existentialist* or an *essentialist*. We are either
"orphaned" *from* our ground of being, or we turn all
our yearning and striving *toward* our ground of
being. The essentialist is "alone, but not lonely." The
existentialist is *not* "alone" (that is, he must inevitably
share with others the existential necessities of life and
destiny), yet *is* "lonely," for he knows no higher reality than his own empirical self, which, together with
other selves, seems simply to have been tossed into
existence. . . . Those for whom the empirical self
serves as center and apex of their soul life cannot
know the sphere of being-above-the-self—the sphere
whence their self first emerged, and which remains
ever its home. [9–10]

According to Tomberg, such a non-transcendent empirical
self compounds a *mental image* within itself on the basis of
bodily impressions (and memories thereof) along with
temperament, character, and inclinations—all knit together
into a comprehensive, summarizing *abstraction*. But the
"real self" from the sphere of "being-above-the-self" is very
different from all these things:

This real self at the center of our being is not an
abstraction, but the concrete reality of the inner identity at our core—that which threads together our life
experiences into one continuous tapestry. Our real self
(not some abstraction of it) is the inner "lord" that
stands *above* the ever-shifting conditions of our soul
life (with its moods, inclinations, wishes, and kaleido-

145

scope of mental images), and that, for the most part, rules over them. This real self is the centerpoint of our soul life, its invariable core. [10]

For this reason, however, the real self was, for Tomberg,

a fragment of Being [*Sein*] fixed within the tumult of our soul's mutable existence [*Dasein*]. Our real self, then, stands at the threshold of two worlds: the world of external existence, and the world of being-above-the-self.

Whereas the existentialist experiences the self in its relation to the external world, the essentialist experiences the self in relation to the world of being-above-the-self. For the existentialist, the self is the experiential *terminus* or final outcome of interiorizing the existential world. For the essentialist, the self is the *point of departure* for an "exodus" into the realm of Being. This latter is the path taken by those intent on becoming ever more essential. Angelus Silesius meant this path when he said: "Man, become essential!" [10–11]

It is this path, too, that Tomberg walked in life, and about which he could say from his own experience:

This "becoming essential" begins with the self, and progresses then through stages of increasing depth and inwardness, until it arrives at what is both the final and the first inwardness: Being, itself, as the source of self—or, *God*. God is not *external* to the self, but is above—transcends—the self. God is the most inward of the inward. God is more inward even than the sanctuary of our own self: for just as our own *self* is inner "lord" of our own *soul*, so is *God* LORD

146

of *all selves*. . . . For the essentialist, God is not a
thing, not an object of knowledge or belief that stands
over against (or, face-to-face with) a knowing subject
or faithful seeker. No, He is beyond and above any
such separation of subject and object: God transcends
both what is objective and what is subjective. [10–11]

This fact is the reason why it is impossible to prove the
existence of God using empirical and scientific means:

The certitude of God's reality that we call "faith" is
not founded upon empiricism, or upon any proof supposed to take its start from empirical reality. Faith is
the *effect* on our self of the reality of God-above-the-
self. God's reality makes itself known by a *breath*
moving through our self, like a homeward wind. This
is not knowledge, for no object is thereby known by a
knowing subject. It would be more true to say that it
is the self, the subject, that is known (or, cognitively
permeated) by higher Being. The self becomes an
object of the all-pervasive cognition of One who is
higher, who transcends the self. [11–12]

The partly lyrical choice of words here points to the fact
that Tomberg is describing his own soul-experiences. Only
because this divine "breath moving through our self, like a
homeward wind" had, over the course of his life, become
more and more a matter of personal certainty, was it possible for him to formulate—retrospectively—the "fundamental tenet of the spiritual stream of essentialism":

Just as the self is both center and "lord" (*kyrios*) of
our soul, so God is both center and LORD (*kyrios*) of
the self, and center of all selves. God as Sun of eternal
Being sends forth His rays of essence into existence,

147

and these rays of essence—as present in existence—are no other than individual selves fashioned in His image and likeness.

Just as the *soul* (with its powers of thinking, feeling, and will) "acknowledges as its lord the self and its revelation," which is *conscience* (except in cases of madness, moral idiocy, or intoxication), so does the *self* "acknowledge as its LORD the God-above-the-self and His revelation," which is *the conscience of consciences* (for this revelation stands *above* individual conscience). [12]

Thus does Tomberg find his way to an unaccustomed definition of the holy:

And it is precisely this conscience of consciences, towering above the individual self and its personal conscience, that, when experienced and recognized as such, is worshipped as *holy* by the self, and also by the powers of the soul subordinated to the self. What is holy to the self is, then, on the one hand, something that is not dissimilar to it by nature, and, on the other, something experienced as towering above it and far surpassing it. [12]

With the help of such insights as these it becomes possible, for example, to understand the command "I am the LORD thy God, which have brought thee out of the land of Egypt, of the house of bondage. Thou shalt have no other gods before me":

The guiding principle of essentialism is *alignment with the holy*, with worshipping the God-above-the-self. As such, it is not a matter of aligning with or worshipping the god alongside or external to the self—and never mind the god below the self! The holy is not to be sought and found in the realm of empirical existence, but in the realm of *Being*: that Being which towers above the self.

Now, the *horizontal* of empirical existence (all that which spatial extension and temporal succession have to offer) can divert and hinder us on the vertical of the path to the God-above-the-self. This is why the revelation of God as Being (Exodus 3:14–15)—as both I AM THE I AM and THE ONE WHO IS— must be *preceded* by an "exodus" from the "house of bondage," an exodus from the polytheistic influences of untold gods laying claim on our piety. Yes, such a revelation must surely be preceded by a "wandering through the desert." That is why the revelation on Mt. Sinai had to come *after* the exodus out of Egypt (and after the subsequent wanderings).

Egypt at that time was a catch-all of cultic attachments to the elemental powers of empirical existence, both in space (sun, moon, and stars) and time (fertility, procreation, life and death, natural evolution)— that is, of devotion directed solely to natural powers representing a full spectrum of the *compulsive* aspects of existence.

But Egypt was a house of bondage not solely on account of the compulsory labor exacted from the Israelites by their masters; this was also (and especially) because the form of worship pervading the land entailed a pleading for the necessities of life from "gods" of empirical existence. For this reason, the exodus of the Israelites out of Egypt was a revolu-

tionary event without precedent. Consider for a
moment: a great multitude chose to go into the desert
to offer sacrifice to a God not present *anywhere* in the
realm of empirical existence, whose name meant
THE ONE WHO IS! This unprecedentedness was,
in fact, precisely Pharaoh's view of the desert exodus.
[13–14]

⊕

Tomberg, who, as a man of the twentieth century, ascends
Mt. Sinai with Moses, not only finds there (in the "world
chronicle") content corresponding to the biblical account
(thus enabling him to bring what occurred there closer to
conceptions current in our own time), but acquires also an
overview of the whole psychological and spiritual situation
of his own century. From this vantage-point, it can be seen
that the totalitarian regimes of three thousand years ago
(e.g., Egypt) and those of today (Tomberg names the Soviet
Union, still then in existence) do not differ in essence. It
also becomes clear that the reality of the "house of bondage" has grown even more comprehensive in the present
day, and clearly goes well beyond the social and political
structure of a state. It is expressed, for example,

in every form of thought or belief that is to any
degree tinged with *determinism*. Whenever we hold to
the belief that chains of causality—set in motion in
the past—inexorably determine not only present
events but also all *future* events, we are confined
within this house of bondage. Whenever we subscribe to the belief that no "uncaused" cause can be
found such as might strike like lightning from the
realm of moral-spiritual freedom into the prevailing

150

world of causality, we are inmates within the walls of this deterministic house of bondage.

Further, belief in determinism is tantamount to *dis*belief in miracles. And whoever does not believe in miracles—and therefore does not believe in the irruption of *new* causes from the moral-spiritual into the existential realm—is *ipso facto* caught in this deterministic house of bondage. Prisoners of this house of bondage hold, for example, that heredity is more powerful than spiritual-moral freedom. For them, heredity is a god before whom they bow down. Thus speaks the determinist: "We are determined by heredity; heredity created us."

Then again, other prisoners of the deterministic house of bondage look to stellar influences (say, in the birth horoscope) as the causal agents of our destinies. For them, the stars also are gods before whom they bow down. As for those who worship natural evolution as a goddess (and their number is legion), they hold that with the aid of its twin protagonists—the struggle for existence and the survival of the fittest—natural evolution contrived to transmogrify an intricate system of nerves and brain into what is called the human being (*homo sapiens*). Those who think this way bow down also before the gods of existence. They do not worship the God-above-the-self. Instead, they worship forces *outside* and *beneath* the self—forces "above in heaven," "below on the earth," or "in the water under the earth."

All who hold such views as we have mentioned here are "in Egypt, in the house of bondage," for they serve the gods of existence and do not acknowledge

151

THE ONE WHO IS, the God of Being. They have not as yet set forth from the house of bondage into the desert to experience there the reality of the God-above-the-self, whose name is THE ONE WHO IS. The encounter with the reality of the God-above-the-self is possible only in the "desert," only beyond the sphere of influence of the other "gods": the gods of *existence*. This is why the first commandment of essentialism proclaims that to acknowledge the God of Being, the God-above-the-self, *precludes* acknowledging any other gods (*elohim aherim*) next to Him. [15–16]

And this is why, as Tomberg further explains,

this claim on our undivided devotion is not satisfied when, for example, such disproportionate prominence is ascribed to the sex drive, or *libido*, that the phenomena of spiritual and cultural life are regarded as little, if anything, more than sublimations of that drive. Far from worshipping the God of Being, those who have fallen victim to this obsession are instead worshipping the ancient goddess Venus (known also as Aphrodite or Astarte), who dominates their every thought and deed. Such people are indeed worshippers of the goddess Venus, no matter how scientifically enlightened they may otherwise believe themselves to be.

Then there are others among the "well-informed" who believe they have located the driving force of evolution in the *struggle for existence*, and the conflicts of class and race that follow from it. Those obsessed in this way are in truth worshippers of Mars.

Thus do the ancient gods reappear disguised in the present! Even inhuman Moloch is back again in the guise of *collectivism*, still demanding human sacrifice as in olden days. Are not collectives (whether of state, national, or class origin) demanding, yet again, that we sacrifice our "firstborn": our heritage, our hereditary rights? In the final analysis, collectives always demand the sacrifice of our individualism. Does not the ancient Phoenician cult of the Canaanites and the Carthaginians live robustly on today in the "worship" of state, party, and national collectives? [17]

Tomberg does not deny that these gods and idols correspond to the actual lived realities of human beings today. Why, then, is it nevertheless so important for him to distinguish from this the God-above-the-self?

Lest our stance on the matters detailed above may seem overwrought, we hasten to emphasize that, for us, the point is not whether such "other gods" actually do correspond "in some way" to existential reality, but that they do not "proceed from" the spheres above the self. They proceed, rather, from the existential spheres *beneath* and *outside* the self. They enslave the self and impede its way to true freedom: to freedom in God, to freedom in He who "is more myself than I myself am." Such "other gods" do not lie on the essentializing vertical of ever-increasing inwardization—that is, on the trajectory from subjective conscience to objective good, from individual self to the fountainhead whence every self shines forth.

God is not just "one phenomenon" among others. *God is the fountainhead of selfhood!* He is more inti-

153

mate, more inward, than the most intimate and inward we know: our own self. For this reason, even taken together, the entirety of the phenomenal world, of the conceptual world of mental images, and of language (to the degree that it conforms to these things) does not suffice to know the God-above-the-self and to bring Him to expression! Only in the *language of the self*, which is the language of conscience, can we conceive of and speak about God. Only in this language can the first and fundamental commandment of essentialism as proclaimed by Moses be heard, understood, and acknowledged: "I am the LORD (*anochi* YHVH), thy God (*elohecha*), who brought you out of the land of Egypt, out of the house of bondage." (Exodus 20:2) In other words: "I am THE ONE WHO IS, who stands above your self, who has freed you from the bondage of existence. That is why you should not fall back into the bondage of existence by subordinating your self to the *forces* of existence!" Or, as Moses records it: "You shall have no other gods besides me." (Exodus 20:3) [17–18]

The distinction between the various gods and the God-above-the-self is, thus, that between slavery and freedom.

Now, it might be objected that Yahweh too—the God of the Israelites—was a national god, like the other gods. Tomberg meets this objection. At the conclusion of his text, he poses the question of the nature of Yahweh-Elohim and of the relation that subsists between Him and the divine Trinity:

Who is YHVH-ELOHIM? Who is the Revealer on Mt. Sinai? Who is the Partner of the covenant with

Israel? Is the Godhead of the world—is the Creator, Redeemer, and Interiorizer of the world; or again, is the eternal Holy Trinity of Father, Son, and Holy Spirit—identical with YHVH, the LORD of the community of Israel? [129]

To answer this question, Tomberg explores the reality of the beings of the heavenly hierarchies, of the "angels" and their various "choirs," with which, as a thirty-year-old, he had already concerned himself in his first published anthroposophical text.[3] First, he notes:

the answer is: yes and no. This contradiction can be resolved by way of synthesis if we recall that, in essence, the religion of Israel was and remains a *prophetic* religion, a religion founded upon the revelation of the prophets. . . . Now, Scripture teaches that prophetic missions are not limited to humankind, but that they extend as well to beings of the spiritual hierarchies, often called "angels" for short. Thus, the first meeting of Moses with God took place when, in the vicinity of Mt. Horeb in the land of Midian, He revealed Himself to Moses by calling to him through the intercession of an angel: "And the angel of the LORD appeared to him in a flame of fire out of the midst of a bush. . . . When the LORD saw that he turned aside to see, God called to him out of the bush: 'Moses, Moses!'" (Exodus 3:2–4)

The angel of the LORD was in the burning bush, and through that angel God called out: "Moses,

---

[3] "The Gospel of St. John as a Way Toward Understanding the Spiritual Hierarchies," *Russian Spirituality*, 1–12.

Moses!" When that angel called Moses by name, it did so as hierarchical bearer and emissary of the LORD. . . . When proclaiming from the burning bush, then, the angel of the LORD spoke and acted in a manner similar to that of human prophets, who likewise speak and act, not from themselves, but from the Being of God-above-the-self Who fills and rules them. . . . Looked at this way (which is quite in keeping with Christian tradition), we must answer in the affirmative the question whether the God of Abraham, Isaac, and Jacob (who also revealed Himself to Moses near Mt. Horeb) is the same as the trinitarian God of Christianity. But looked at another way—taking into consideration especially the role Scripture grants prophets and hierarchical beings as representatives of the Divine—the angel of the LORD (to take one example) who spoke from the burning bush *in the name of* the God of Abraham, Isaac, and Jacob was clearly *just* an angel and *not* the God of Abraham, Isaac, and Jacob Himself.

Just as Moses's mission to lead the people of Israel out of Egypt was proclaimed from the burning bush by an angelic being, so did another hierarchical being—delegated to this task by the Most High—proclaim the ten commandments to Moses from the dark cloud amid flashes of lightning and peals of thunder. And it was *this* hierarchical being Who entered into the covenant with the people of Israel in the name, and on behalf of, the Most Holy One. [129–31]

In this meditation on the role of the beings of the higher spiritual hierarchies, Tomberg points to a realization which is important to him: that the various angels each have quite

156

individual essential characteristics. This is true also of Yahweh:

> YHVH-ELOHIM exhibits individual features characteristic of hierarchical beings, just as Elijah (to take one example) exhibits individual features characteristic of human beings. For even though their missions are divine, both wonder-working and proclaiming "prophets" (whether human or hierarchical beings) exhibit an *individual* character. When Moses shattered the stone tablets, this was no part of fulfilling his prophetic mission of proclaiming the ten commandments, but solely an expression of his individual indignation at the revolt staged at the foot of Mt. Sinai by those worshipping the golden calf. Similarly, such biblical descriptions of YHVH-ELOHIM's actions as His punishing decrees as the "jealous God" (imposed out of anger, and later revoked) show that, in fulfilling the task set Him by the eternal Holy Trinity, YHVH-ELOHIM nonetheless had leeway to express His individual nature. [131–32]

And it is precisely by this irreplaceably individual element that the hierarchical rank of Yahweh can be recognized:

> Indeed, the particular features of YHVH-ELOHIM's individual nature, as depicted in the Bible, even suggest to which rank of the spiritual hierarchies He belongs. That rank is made plain in the biblical episodes of His characteristic mode of action: demonstrating His *power*. We see this first in the transformation of the rod of Moses into a snake that swallows the snakes created by the Egyptian priests in a similar manner. Next come the ten plagues inflicted

upon Egypt, and then the destruction of Pharaoh's army in the Red Sea. Clearly, the argument that should have convinced Pharaoh and the Egyptians to let the Israelites go was that they had on their side a mighty, invisible ally who wielded such power over the elements that it was senseless to resist His will! . . .

We have already emphasized that YHVH's *modus operandi* during the captivity of the people of Israel in Egypt, as well as during their exodus out of Egypt, is characterized in the Bible as the manifestation of *power*, a power extending all the way to the elements of nature. This fact alone indicates that YHVH is not a being of the lowest hierarchy (angels, archangels, and archai), because their field of activity is the role of conscience. We need only consider the biblical accounts to discover that no effect on Pharaoh's conscience, or on the conscience of the Egyptian people, was ever attributed to YHVH; and similarly, that the empowering factor for the exodus of the Israelites out of Egypt had nothing whatsoever to do with kindling Pharaoh's conscience to let them go, or with inspiring the Egyptians' insight into the Israelite people's right to leave Egypt. No, what in fact enabled the exodus were the ten plagues inflicted upon the land, and the destruction of the Egyptian army in the waters of the Red Sea.

In other words, the exodus of the people of Israel was made possible by nothing other than the manifestation of YHVH's power over the elements of nature. Now, from the fact that the hierarchical rank of the *powers* or *exusiai* (of the second hierarchy) rules the elements of nature, and is as well (when so authorized from above) empowered to influence natural events, it follows that YHVH—as the fully empowered hierarchical representative, proclaimer, and wonderworking "prophet" of the Most High, is a being of the second hierarchy belonging in fact to the rank of the powers (*exusiai*). It was, then, a being of this rank Who, as God's representative, entered into the special covenantal relationship with the community of Israel and became the providential leader and architect of its path of destiny. [136–37]

⊕

If we consider carefully the above explanations offered by Tomberg (which represent only a small excerpt from the text)—from the events in the dark cloud, to essentialism, to the way of the desert, and to the being of Yahweh-Elohim—we begin to see in a quite new light the question he asked in Bad Godesberg, and then in Mülheim ("How does divine law become human law-giving?"), and that we are in fact able to answer it. To do so, we must first commit ourselves to the path of searching for the divine source. This search consists of two "stretches of road." The first, horizontal, stretch, leads inwards from peripheral matters, from being bound up with the outside world, into our own center: this is the "way of the desert," which means a transition from existentialism to essentialism. The second stretch consists in turning from the horizontal to the vertical. It takes its point of departure from our own inner center, and leads upwards into the God-above-the-self. The people of Israel trod the first stretch, which leads to the vertical genesis of law on behalf of all humanity; the second stretch, the ascent itself, was reserved to Moses as an individual, alone.

The vertical process of the genesis of law proves to be a three-stage process, just as Tomberg had earlier postulated in his jurisprudential work. That is, the *eternal* and immutable law (*lex aeterna*)—which is the very essence of God—is revealed by Yahweh-Elohim, a being from the *divine* hierarchy of *powers*, as divine law (*lex divina*). With the help of His power over the elements of *nature*, Yahweh-Elohim then adapts this law to the nature of human beings in such a way ("amid thunder and lightning") that it had necessarily to appear to them as if in "a dark cloud on a high mountain," while yet being recognizable to the most advanced among them. In Moses's consciousness (which had been rendered perfect by means of the clarifying and purifying "way of the desert"), what took place in the cloud on the mountain was reflected in such a way that he was able to "translate" the divine archetypes thus communicated to him by Yahweh into human language. Moses brings the law expressed in this way, apportioned to the true nature of human beings (*lex naturalis*), down from the mountain into the *human* life-world in the form of the ten commandments, where it becomes the positive law which is in force (*lex humana*). In the particular case of the people of Israel, this positive law is embodied in (among other sources) the legal regulations recorded in the Torah in AD 613.

⊕

With Tomberg's spiritual ascent of Sinai, moreover, two other circles were closed. The first circle spans his life from the beginning of his work as an anthroposophical author to his mature description of the angelic choirs and of the individual angels—in particular Yahweh-Elohim—in which respect for the life's work of Rudolf Steiner plays a central part. The second circle covers his "second life," from his work on three-stage law immediately after his abandonment of Anthroposophy and departure from Holland, through to his demonstration—in this, his last completed text—that three-stage law is indeed of *divine* origin.

The late Tomberg, however, knows *also* that the origin of three-stage law (as it becomes evident in the ten commandments) *cannot* be demonstrated by "legal" (jurisprudential) means, since a *different* language is manifest in it: the language of essentialism and love; the language of the self. For this reason, Tomberg concludes his last completed text with the following words:

> The ten commandments are a reflection of the splendor of the world-order. They are an expression of *truth* that is, as it were, crystallized in them. Just as the multivalence of the soul's life of imagination, feeling, and will has a central focus around which it orders and orients itself, so too does the peripheral multiplicity of cosmic manifestation as a whole have *one* central focus that orders and holds everything together. And just as the human self is the centerpoint of the plurality of the soul's manifestations, so is the *one* God-above-the-self the centerpoint of the world. The plurality of cosmic manifestation may be likened to a periphery; and its unity may be likened to the *center* of that periphery. Now, that center—which holds together the periphery of multiform cosmic manifestation, giving it meaning and direction—is no other than the very Self of the cosmos. And as for that peripheral multiplicity of cosmic manifestation, it can form no *image* of the God-above-the-self. Neither

can the peripheral multiplicity of cosmic manifestation proclaim His name. For the *unimaginable* and *unnameable* God-above-the-self can *only* be recognized and named in the language of the self. But the self's own language is that of *love*. The human self speaks only *in* love and *through* love; otherwise it remains silent. Love is the life-element of the soul, its substance, its power of growth. Love is also the source of certainty concerning God's presence in the world, for it is the bond of love that unites the self with God. Love recognizes God, just as the human self is recognized *by* God. [126–27]

⊕

It is this *primordial language of the self and of love* that Valentin Tomberg sought to speak, both orally and in writing; and which he sought to deepen. In its element, he was "wholly at home"; here, he could show his true nature. This language governed not only his vertical orientation to God and the spiritual world, but prevailed in a special way also among his close family and in the few intense friendships they kept up.